the

# hairy

book of

email

© 2017 Philip Jackson

Get in touch: phil@buildyoursalon.uk

### Dedication

For my Mum.  Everyone should have someone in their life who is always proud.

| | |
|---|---|
| Introduction | i |
| Disclaimer | iii |
| Preface | iv |

## PART ONE

## Email for beginners

| | |
|---|---|
| Why email? | 2 |
| The 7 ways we can use email in our salons | 14 |
| How to send your emails | 17 |
| Types of email | 21 |

## PART TWO

## Understanding your Database

| | |
|---|---|
| Your database | 33 |
| Your database, segmented | 37 |
| Growing your Email List | 45 |
| Your Sending Schedule | 54 |
| Planning your Campaigns | 61 |
| A Word on Unsubscribes | 66 |
| Measuring success | 69 |
| Layout, format and tone | 74 |
| The Dark Art of Subject Lines | 80 |
| The Body of your Email | 87 |

## PART THREE

### The Interviews

| | |
|---|---|
| Neil Prigent - Jas Hair | 97 |
| Alex Quinn - Phorest | 104 |
| Jo Burgess - Shortcuts | 114 |
| Bart Foreman - Endgame Marketing Solutions | 126 |
| Chris Davis - ActiveCampaign | 136 |

## ACKNOWLEDGEMENTS
## SPECIAL OFFERS - WORTH £674!

# Introduction

**I LOVE marketing.** And I love salons too. This means that salon marketing is always on my radar and I probably notice it more than your average person. I can't help myself! I'm always peering into salon windows when they are closed, both at home and when I'm on holiday. I can lose hours being nosey about what other salons are doing online, how they position themselves and how they advertise. For a real treat, take a look at some of the salon ads in your local paper: they are very often a great example of terrible copywriting, if nothing else!

**I am also a bloody CHEAPSKATE**, as my friends will attest. Actually, that's not true - I *love* to spend money, but I absolutely hate to *waste* money. Feeling conned or that I am not getting great value annoys me immensely and making poor choices about how to spend salon cash will keep me awake at night. And trust me, I've made some dreadful advertising decisions: newspaper ads that didn't deliver (my fault for not checking the demographics), event sponsorship in the £000s (my fault as that was before I learnt to say 'no'), radio advertising with zero return (again my fault, but the sales guy was so *very* cute).

**I love technology.** Since the days of the BBC B home computer, via the Sega Master System and into the first hand-held organisers (remember Psion?), I've been a tech junkie for years. I suppose then that email marketing for salons was inevitable for me. Something that enabled me to shout about how great my salon is, a tool to promote our staff and services, at a relatively low cost and generating big returns: perfect!

**FINALLY, I love a drink.** I'm lucky to have a fair few salon owners in my social circle: they seem to like a drink too. It was during one boozy evening in the period of time I was writing this book that I was shocked to learn about how little email marketing was being done by my friends. Some couldn't see *why* they should be marketing this way, most could see the benefits but didn't have the time, more knew they *should* be doing it but didn't know where to start. Hence this book: I hope that by the end of your lunch hour (yes, I'm being sarcastic - I know that salon owners never get a full lunch hour) you'll know *why* email marketing has become a vitally important marketing pillar in my business, you'll know what to send, who to and how often.

I hope this little book serves you well. Even if you decide to do nothing with the information it will give you a better idea of what *might* be done and how easy most of it is. It should protect you from a sneaky attack from the so-called "experts" who like to circle our beloved industry sniffing for blood. Also please keep in touch. I love hearing about how salon owners and managers are nailing it in this amazing industry.

Phil Jackson
buildyoursalon.com

## Disclaimer

I do not believe in success without hard work. My books and programmes are designed to inspire you to take action, in conjunction with other efforts to grow your business. As required by law, I make no guarantees about your ability to get results or earn any money with my ideas, information, tools or strategies. All books, products and services are for entertainment, educational and informational purposes only. I don't know you or your business, so nothing I say constitutes a promise or guarantee of specific results, outcomes or future earnings. I do not offer any legal, medical, tax or other professional advice. Where I share results I do so only to illustrate concepts and these results should not be considered potential earnings, exact figures, or promises of actual or future performance. Do not make any decisions based on any information presented in my books, products, events, services, or web site, without understanding that making any change in your business or personal life is accompanied by the risk of hardship or significant losses. Exercise extreme caution and seek advice from trusted, qualified professionals before attempting any lifestyle change or business or financial endeavour. Check with your medical doctor, qualified accountant, lawyer or indemnified professional advisor, before acting on this or any information. Continuing with this book indicates your agreement that you will not to attempt to hold me liable for your decisions, actions or results, at any time, under any circumstance.

# Preface

Who here is baffled by email marketing? Many salons now have some kind of computerised reception system: maybe you've got your reception system set up but you don't feel you're using it to its full potential? Wouldn't it be great to get a little more out of your investment? Or maybe you just want to make sure every possible marketing pillar is in place and you're maximising the potential of your salon business.

Since my first book, *The Hairy Book of Innovation*, was published I've been privileged to have a good nose around lots of salon businesses as either a mentor or consultant. You have no idea what a joy it is to see inside other salon businesses without being emotionally involved! The joy of mentoring is that a little detachment from problems often makes finding great solutions so much easier: I strongly recommend finding a business mentor as soon as possible (don't wait until times are hard, and definitely not for the next economic downturn: coaches and mentors will have little free time!).

Much like business networking, when you take a look at other salons across the country, even across the world, you very quickly realise that no matter what a salon is charging, no matter what their town is like and no matter what the salon owner's ambitions are, we fundamentally have the same challenges:

- staff (too many, too few, can't find them, not motivated, absenteeism, stealing products, hangovers, etc.)
- suppliers (no support, poor sales reps, unfair contracts, competing for tight profit margins, etc.), and
- customers (too few of them, not spending enough, poor loyalty, etc.)

Almost as an afterthought, I started to notice one little detail on my visits: how much salon owners *love* to spend money on their reception systems. Beautiful, modern PCs and Macs, their touch screens glistening with oils and serums, specs far superior to what the owners had at home and very often accompanied by hefty monthly invoices from their chosen software supplier.

My visit was not usually connected to external marketing, but I'm inquisitive (or nosy) by nature so I chatted to salon owners about how they used their systems.

At worst, the thousands that had been invested in IT sat on reception as a glorified appointment book: literally you could have swapped that touchscreen for a paper diary and the business wouldn't have changed one jot. In fact in one salon I found the only person getting any *real* utility out of the system was the apprentice who was using the computer to type up the written assignments for her beauty therapy qualification.

A fair few salons were getting a little more bang for their buck by using online bookings to populate the appointment system, SMS appointment reminders, etc. and a pleasing number were getting some useful management reports to help set targets for their team.

There was a very small number of salons (I'd say less than 10%) using their systems to market regularly to their customers. Of those, more than half were using only SMS marketing. That leaves around 4% of salons carrying out *any* email marketing at all. I'm also sorry to say that the email marketing I did see was pretty uninspiring: usually poorly written, often bland and uninteresting and very rarely sent with any kind of expectation in mind at all.

This book is for the salon owner that likes to feel they are getting *value for money*: it's high time that beautiful reception system earned its place on the desk!

I am not, of course, suggesting that salons should rely on email marketing and ignore all other methods. In the same way as one shade of hair colour won't suit all of your current and potential customers, neither will one flavour of marketing suit them all either. Think of your salon as the Parthenon in Athens: the more marketing pillars you have in place the more your salon can shine as a beacon, a destination, a landmark. What I'm submitting is that most salons:

- aren't sending enough emails
- aren't targeting those emails correctly
- are sending dull, uninteresting content

- aren't turning emails into cash in the till

I work with salons to help them achieve bigger profits and I have worked with salons of all sizes, hair or beauty or both and on different continents, but I have yet to start working with a salon that already had a robust email marketing strategy in place. It seems our industry has become obsessed with social media marketing[1], so much so that we are neglecting other important ways of reaching out to our current and potential customers.

I've been the owner of Bravo Hairdressing in the south of England for 15 years and for many of those years we'd been fairly successful. We weren't exactly blazing a trail but we were doing OK. We worked hard, our earnings were pretty good too: certainly more than we could have been paid working elsewhere in our town. If I'm honest I probably didn't think of myself as a business owner at all and I know I wasn't alone when kidding myself that the salon industry was somehow a different animal, unique in the commercial world with profoundly different challenges.

My journey has been a shift in paradigm: moving from being a busy stylist and salon owner to a business owner, manager and mentor. Over the years I've got my salon to the stage where it needs me less and less. I've

---

[1] By the way anyone who thinks email marketing is dead in favour of social media should try signing up for a Facebook account without an email address. It's impossible! I predict that email is going to be with us for quite a while yet.

implemented huge changes to bring a systemised approach and I've had to train myself in sales, finance, marketing, web design, copywriting and staff development.

It's been a long and tricky journey and I've made it my job to help other salon owners and managers on their journey too.

Much of my own progress was driven through necessity rather than planning or ambition, as dramatic change often is. In my own business, crunch time hit in 2011 when we adopted my eldest son.

Those who know me will recognise that I am the King of Lists: I love a new project and I count planning and implementation as two of my strongest skills. In my naivety I approached parenting in the same way (I can almost feel the parents reading this sniggering as they read. Don't judge me too harshly, please!).

I have massive respect for all parents but I have particular empathy for those who have chosen to adopt as the process is long, arduous and emotionally draining. Of course, I have no regrets but by the time my Little Dude had moved into our home I was exhausted and had to throw myself 100% into parenting, virtually neglecting my salon business. We'd planned for me to return to work, at least part-time, after LD had been with us at home for six weeks. Unfortunately LD had endured a fairly chaotic start to life and had been moved around a lot: in fact this brave little man had endured more upheaval in his 2½ years than many of us deal with in a lifetime. He needed consistency, stability and time to settle and it was my job to provide it. Very quickly it became apparent that six weeks would be nowhere near enough time for him to adapt, in fact it became a condition of his adoption that I stay home for a minimum of six *months*.

Of course I know how lucky we are and I am very grateful every day for the blessing of parenthood, but in business terms the timing was atrocious. In 2011 the UK was crawling out of the longest, deepest recession we can remember: our customers were struggling and that meant we were really struggling too.

I'm a firm believer in the risk and reward of business: you take the risk and can enjoy the reward. I don't expect my employees to share that risk when times are hard, but neither do I expect them to ask for extra reward when times are good. Bearing in mind that my husband works in the business too and that we both relied on the salon as our sole source of income you can imagine the stress and anxiety that came from us having to skip three paycheques in a row just so we could afford to keep the lights on in the salon and our staff employed.

My accountant estimated that we were just six months away from bankruptcy. Salon. Home. Income. All gone.

We scrimped and we saved, we cut costs wherever we could but nothing seemed to help enough for us to get ahead. Finally I realised that cutting back would never help us enough: we needed more customers in the salon, spending a larger amount of money and with a higher frequency.

I threw myself into learning as much as I could about my business.  Within 18 months we were breaking even again and now, with two wonderful sons at home, we're smashing our own turnover and profit targets month after month and winning awards along the way too - and I'm *still* only working in the salon two days a month.

Essentially what I achieved was to find ways to contribute to the salons financial success of my salon without physically being there and email marketing has been massively important part of that.  It allows me to communicate with my potential and current customers from anywhere in the world and to support my salon and my team without having to come into the salon at all.  I'm not suggesting that you give up working in your own salon: your journey is your own and many of the lifestyle choices I've made may leave you cold. I'm sharing with you the *option*, not the *obligation*, of changing the way you think about what you bring to the table in your business.

What I am going to share with you is a distillation of everything I've learnt from my own experiences and successes and I'm adding in the opinions and insights from some *much* cleverer people too.

"It's time for the salon industry to get in the game with email".

*Phil Jackson*

# PART ONE

## Email for beginners

## Why email?

OK, I admit I am a bit of an email marketing junkie. I'm bewildered why salons don't use this marketing pillar more. There is so much to be gained by engaging with your customers by email and so little to lose, even if it goes horribly wrong. It *will* go wrong, by the way: you may as well get that clear in your head right now. I've sent half-baked emails to people who should never has received them countless times.

> Did my business fail? *No.*
>
> Did anyone die? *No.*
>
> Did the earth spin off its axis? *No.*

I just sent another email either apologising, correcting my error or clarifying what wasn't clear and got on with my day. *Relax*: this is email marketing and certainly not open-heart surgery. In my experience you'd have to be really very offensive to put your salon at risk and the worst outcome is normally that you just miss the mark with your message or promotion. The potential downside is remarkably small but before we get stuck in I think it's important that we enjoy the upside and explore the benefits of using email for a few moments.

> "The benefits of a comprehensive marketing program using marketing automation tools to deliver the right message to the right guest

through the right channel at the right time is a powerful marketing strategy."

*Bart Foreman, Endgame Marketing Solutions*

**It's really low cost – even close to free**

Even if your reception diary isn't computerised, you can begin sending email marketing to your customers without spending a single extra penny (I'm afraid I refuse to count *any* activity that takes any of your precious time as 'free' and I strongly suggest you adopt the same attitude).

"It's a very cheap way of keeping in contact with guests and depending on what you communicate the benefits can be immense."

*Neil Prigent, Jas Salons*

There are lots of email services: though it's not my favourite many small businesses use Mailchimp whose free account will cater to the needs of most. My preference is ActiveCampaign which I find much easier and quicker to navigate, but whatever you decide please *don't* be tempted to send bulk emails from your usual mail program. Mail, Outlook and the like were not designed to send emails to large numbers of contacts and you'll find your account in quite a poor state if you start to get customers trying to unsubscribe from your mailing list. A dedicated bulk mail program also has all of the tools to keep you the right side of all kinds of regulations surrounding data and privacy.

You may already have a computerised reception system capable of sending emails to your customers. If so, you have even *more* reason to start email marketing straight away! Over the years you will spend hundreds or even thousands of pounds with your chosen software provider. It is your duty as a conscientious owner or manager to sweat *every* asset in your business and get more bang for your buck.

Using either a separate program or your existing system will allow you to send thousands of marketing emails a month to your customers, all without spending one extra penny. In time, you might decide to pay a professional copywriter to design your email campaigns for you. Even then, each send will still cost less than an envelope and stamp.

**It's targeted**

Consider advertising a fantastic new organic ready-meal: full of wholesome ingredients, prepared in a way your family will love (even the pickiest 7 year-old) and you can get it from freezer to table in just 10 minutes. If it was your job to advertise this amazing product, how would you do it? Which of these two approaches do you think would give you the best returns?

      a. A glossy advert in a weekly national news magazine, or

b. The same ad in a magazine whose readership targets middle-income, professional mums who are returning to work

Even though the advert in 'a' might have a bigger readership and even yield more sales overall, for a return on your marketing spend I'll wager that 'b' will give you better results: quite simply, targeted marketing works and the closer we can get to a more tailored, intimate conversation with our audience the more effective our marketing becomes.

> "By incorporating personalised messages and sending emails at just the right time, you can create engagement on a very personal level".
>
> *Jo Burgess, Shortcuts*

As you'll see, email marketing allows you to chop your email list in lots of exciting and innovative ways to tailor your conversations with ease.

**Nobody else is doing it**

This I find bewildering, but in my own salon I am rather thankful. If you have ever launched a new website for your salon you'll have seen first hand how cluttered the marketplace is with salon websites. Driving traffic to your website is hard work, requires continual effort and updating and can cost quite a bit in the way of investment and time too. By contrast, try sending a well-thought-out email campaign to your customers: I'll bet very few, if any, emails from salons land in their email Inbox that day.

> "A lot of savvy established businesses do not know how to email their customers regularly."
>
> *Chris Davis, ActiveCampaign*

> "When we started we were among the first to do it and clients were impressed with our professionalism".
>
> *Neil Prigent, Jas Hair Salons*

I doubt this will last forever as those of us who are getting great results with our emails are starting to get noticed. In the mean time, however, enjoy yourself in a relatively uncluttered competitive environment.

**It keeps you in the mind of your customer**

It's not your customer's job to remember to spend money with you: it's your job to remind them. *A lot!*

> "Email marketing is one of the most efficient, measurable and effective ways to market your salon. It's a way for you to stay in touch with your clients and stay front of their minds."
>
> *Alex Quinn, Phorest*

We lead busy lives and salon appointments can very easily fall low in the list of customer priorities.  See if this sounds at all familiar:

- Your customer leaves the salon without rebooking: she forgot her diary, or the parking meter was about to run out or (perish the thought) nobody asked her to rebook as she paid for her services.

- Your customer wakes up a few weeks later realising her hair/skin/whatever is a mess and she really is due to have that service carried out today.

- She calls the salon, can't find an appointment that suits you and her for 10 days.

If you want to really scare yourself, run some figures past your accountant: what would happen if every regular client left it an extra 10 days between each appointment?  The affect on your business could be ruinous.

I can tell you *exactly* how many people respond to an offer I send by email, but harder to measure is the number of people who weren't interested in that *particular* offer, but were still prompted to pick up the phone and book their regular appointment.  Staying current in the mind of your customer is *valuable*: for a more cheery demonstration of the power of frequency, ask your accountant what would happen if you *sped up* the return rate for your regular customers by 7 days or got all your existing customers to make one extra visit to your salon per year.

### It gives you a chance to project your personality

"One of the biggest advantages of email marketing is that you are 100% in control of the message you send out, and who sees it."

*Jo Burgess, Shortcuts*

People buy from people and companies they know, like and trust. Trying to build that familiarity and get the whole spirit of your salon, its personality, attitude, values and beliefs into a 6" x 4" print ad if really, *really* difficult. By contrast, regular email contact gives you bags of opportunity to tell your customers exactly what you're all about over time.

### It's takes no precious salon-time

If you can get online you can set up and send an email marketing campaign from anywhere in the world. The joy of this kind of activity for me is I can squeeze it between putting the kids in bed and my husband getting home from work, into an extended lunch break or into a slot left by a last-minute cancellation. I've sent emails from coffee shops, from the Plymouth to London Paddington train, from a cabana by a pool in Las Vegas, from airline lounges, even from the school car park while I waited for my children to come back from an excursion.

I'm very reluctant to sacrifice the few precious hours I spend in the salon so I try to schedule all my marketing emails at the beginning of each month then get on with the rest of my work, but if there's a little time and a decent internet connection I'm ready to send wherever the mood takes me and the opportunity occurs.

**It helps your other marketing hit harder**

Any marketing is more powerful when its seen as part of a larger marketing strategy, but even at its most basic level you can run a basic money-off promotion on conditioning treatments in-salon and with a little time and effort get some kind of response. Back that promotion with an email extolling the virtues of a conditioning treatment during the summer months which the customer has read a week before her appointment and I'll bet my last *penny* that your response will be stronger.

I see salon owners make the mistake of trying to run all of their marketing pillars in the same way as their social media: they simply shout the same message in five different ways. Embrace the differences and play to the strengths of each platform where you can.

> "Use social media to amplify, to build a following, get your message out there, but once it's out there you need to capture those people. You do that by getting their email addresses, taking a conversation offline, in the email box. That's intimate, quiet and individualised."
>
> *Chris Davis, ActiveCampaign*

**It's easy to track**

I hope by now you've stopped spending money on marketing where you can't prove its effectiveness. Spending hard-earned salon cash on *any* form of advertising or marketing which can't be tracked is a fast way to make a loss. Technology is your friend here. There are ways to monitor the returns on every press ad, flyer drop and online promotion, but measuring the success of e-mail marketing is amongst the easiest.

You can see at a glance how many emails were sent, how many were opened and how many clicked the lovely clear call-to-action you included. No guesswork. This means you can scale or repeat the promotions that were effective while editing or abandoning those that failed to gain any traction. I *promise* this is easier than it sounds!

**It's not invasive**

This one takes a little getting used to as a marketing concept. In my consultancy work I have encountered a lot of resistance from salon owners and managers who feel that somehow marketing by email is an invasion of privacy.

You need to get any doubts around this out of your mind *now*. Of course, we must respect the privacy of our customers but I think it is helpful to see email marketing in the context of the alternatives available.

Instead of emailing, you might choose to send physical mailings to your customers at home. There is a place for direct mail in your overall marketing strategy but my own experience as a salon owner tells me that customers tend to be more comfortable giving their email address, particularly in the early stages of a client relationship, than they are their mailing address. My suspicion is that customers also feel that unsubscribing (should they choose not to receive your wonderful marketing in future) is a relatively easy process compared to removing yourself from a physical mailing list: a couple of clicks, and they're done.

Compare email marketing also with SMS marketing. There is a strong case for using SMS in our salons: I don't know of any salon which has not seen a reduction in the number of customer no-shows through sending SMS reminders a day or two before an appointment. This kind of timely, transactional contact is perfect for SMS but I've also seen unsubscribe rates far outpace email unsubscribes when you start sending SMS marketing to your customers on a frequent basis. Though open rates are incredibly high and responses can be lightning-fast, in my experience customers seem to feel SMS is *far* more invasive and aggravating than email. SMS demands immediate attention and very often receives it, where email is opened in your own time.

I'd also add the sending of 'Push' notifications to this category of thinking. Interrupting someone's day with a marketing 'Push' is a really quick way to get them to either delete your app or at least to turn your notifications off. Interestingly, the content of the marketing message seems to pale into insignificance, at least for some audiences. The intrusion outweighs any benefit they may have received from the message you are sending.

**Emails hang around**

If you want to distribute information that a customer can go back and refer to later, email is hard to beat. SMS messages aren't always very easy to search through and tend to be very quickly or even immediatetely deleted. If a customer finds an email interesting it is often kept and opened more than once, particularly if the first open was on a mobile device.

**Emails support your online presence**

The chances are very high that your customer will open your emails on a mobile device. The joy of using email, as opposed to postal mail for example, is that you can lead your customer to other online resources. Your customer is in clicking mode when they are checking emails so it's a straightforward click to show your customer your Facebook page, send them to make a purchase at your online shop, direct them to your online booking portal, etc. Trying to drive traffic to these online resources from an offline ad in your local newspaper or from a billboard is much harder: your potential customers aren't in clicking mode when they see your ad!

"Staying connected with salon guests is the strategy we want to focus on. The delivery tactic may be postal (snail) mail that costs a lot, texting, phone apps, or social media channels. Email is the most powerful of these tactics but it does not and should not be viewed in isolation."

Bart Foreman, Endgame Marketing Solutions

**Email is fun!**

OK. I have a tendency to geek out a little bit. You might think I'm sad. I don't care. Crafting a beautiful, thoughtful email campaign that *works* is a wonderful feeling. When I am writing an email that I think will deliver great results, something I've researched and thought about for a while, I've read and re-read to get my message polished and honed, then it's time to hit 'send', in that moment I feel like I am genuinely in the driving seat of my business and steering its success. There's nowhere to hide and nobody else to blame. And I love it. When I check later that day and my campaign has started turning into extra cash in my till I really couldn't be happier.

Join me! Let's geek out together for a while!

> "Email marketing is going nowhere ... We're just going to continue to build on its effectiveness."

Chris Davis, ActiveCamaign

## The 7 ways we can use email in our salons

As with any marketing activity, it's really important that we identify exactly what it is that we want our email marketing to achieve. Without this clarity your marketing tends to be rather blunt, woolly and ineffective.

Personally I don't try to achieve too much in each email. You'll see later on that my emails tend to be short, snappy and chatty rather than huge, long sales pages. I think there are seven potential objectives for an email: I would avoid the temptation of trying to hit more than one or two points in each email to keep your message really clear.

1. First up, email can help you build your salon brand. If we communicate with a consistent voice our emails can help communicate what we are about: help us share our attitudes, our values and our brand personality. This is a kind of over-arching objective: you want this in every email alongside the other objectives.

"My biggest piece of advice (other than finding the right technology!) for anyone who is feeling like email marketing is just too difficult, is to inject as much personality as they can into what they do.

Jo Burgess, Shortcuts

You can send emails that are purely to communicate your brand: for example, you might send a news piece telling your customers about a charity initiative you've been supporting and use the email to communicate your values. This would be perfectly valid, but don't expect a lot of response: even if your customers are really interested and lots of them read the piece few of them are likely to reply.

2. We can use emails to ask for referrals. You can do this on a continual basis throughout the year (I have worked with salons who trigger this campaign after a customer's third visit to the salon, for example) or in my own salon I prefer to run an annual 'recommend-a-friend' campaign by email every August.

3. We can use email to send people to your website, online bookings portal or blog. We call this 'generating traffic' for a webpage. This is one of the most common objectives for a marketing email and also one of the easiest to measure your success.

4. We can use emails to help with customer retention. By engaging with our customers regularly we keep their interest and keep us at the front of their minds when they are making a buying decision.

5. We can use emails to communicate offers: to increase the frequency of our customers' visits, to increase their spend when they are in the salon or to

introduce them to new, profitable services and products. This is the obvious one for most salons.

6. We can send emails to people who aren't customers yet to encourage them to begin spending with us. I hardly ever see salons using email marketing in this way which is a shame. There seems to be a mental block which means salon owners can only imagine emailing those customers that they have already sold to. There's a huge opportunity here: you just need to be imaginative about how you get hold of email addresses for people who aren't your customers yet. More on that later.

7. And finally, we can try to get ex-customers back in the salon. For lots of reasons, customers who were one-time visitors or regular customers fall off the radar. We can use email marketing in an effort to remind them that they haven't been forgotten and to give them an excuse to become lovely, loyal customers once again. We call this 'reengagement'.

I hope by now you're realising that there are lots of things we can use email for: it's not all about selling!

## How to send your emails

I'm hoping by now that I've convinced you of the need, or at least the benefit, of sending emails to your customers. Next I want to explore some of the options we have for actually getting our emails out into the world.

At the start you may be tempted to use your personal email account. I see this a lot, particularly with room- or chair-renters, mobile therapists and hairdressers. Please don't! It's really not appropriate for sending any decent quantity of emails and most accounts just aren't set up for it. It's also often against the terms and conditions of some email providers to send commercial or broadcast emails, but most importantly you won't be getting the information and feedback you need to improve your emails over time. A good business email service will show you how many people opened your email, how many people clicked a link inside the email and also efficiently take care of people who don't want to hear from you any more.

If you're lucky enough to have a computerised reception system you will probably want to use that for sending your emails, and I would definitely recommend this for some of your emails (for example appointment reminders). In a lot of systems you can set up these emails then pretty much forget about them (though I would tinker with them occasionally if you are adding any kind of time-sensitive discount or offer too). Your reception system really is the best option for this kind of communication because exporting a list of clients with appointments in 48 hours, importing it into another system and emailing them every day would be an insane waste of time. My biggest bugbear with salon systems, however, is the lack of information you get on the performance of your campaigns. Hardly any will tell you how many people actually opened an email, some will tell you how many bookings you received as a result of a send (which is great for offers and discounts but little use for newsletters or information emails) and frighteningly there are some that give you no information at all: the email literally disappears into the ether and you just keep fingers crossed that it arrived.

I use my computerised reception system for all of my value-adding emails i.e. the ones where I'm just delivering great information. These tend to go out to large sections of my list at once and can be personalised very easily with the information I already have in my system.

If you don't have a computerised reception system the alternative is to signup for a business email service. Some of these you probably heard of before: MailChimp seems to be one of the most popular in our industry (which rather bewilders me) but there are lots of others. My favourite is ActiveCampaign which I think has a much better visual dashboard, plus you can plot out your promotional activity as a logical flowchart. Some companies offer a "Free" plan which lets you have a certain number of contacts saved or send a limited number of emails. I use ActiveCampaign for all of my promotional emails and have for years now.

Before that I used MailChimp and never spent a penny with them! The limits on the free accounts are usually adequate for our needs but the prices for the paid-for systems are really very reasonable. I've also found that some of the paid systems are very much easier to use and save me a lot of time: for the minimal outlay I really think it is money well spent.

If you're going to use an email service I would sign up for lots of free trials before you make up your mind, though it's worth mentioning that email services aren't like your reception system. Most have no minimum term contract so the commitment on your part is usually very small. You can chop and change fairly easily and things in the software market change very quickly: different services become the frontrunner for seemingly short amounts of time before a competitor overtakes.

You've probably realised by now that I use my reception system to send some emails, and I use a separate email service (ActiveCampaign) for others, so what I have to do is take the up-to-date information from my reception system and drop it into my email service. The process is much more straightforward than it sounds. My reception system exports the client data on request. I ask it for a document called a CSV file[2] which is how other bits of software like to read the data. I drop the file into ActiveCampaign and the

---

[2] CSV is 'Comma Separated Value' but don't worry about that. I don't even have to open and look at the file at all

software takes care of the rest for me. If that sounds to daunting or technical, either call your reception system support-line and get them to talk you through at least their half of the equation, or don't do it for now! Learn to use your reception system for the time being and you might even find it does everything you need it to. Additionally, the more we ask for improvements to the mail systems in our salon software, the more the software companies will pay attention and make the changes in future updates.

Before we go any further, I think it's time we got a handle on a little bit of jargon around the types of emails we could be sending.

## Types of email

Think about the emails you receive every day. They don't all look the same, and it isn't just the branding of the sender that changes. The receipt for your latest Amazon purchase, a sales email from a car leasing company and the latest article from your favourite blog writer are very different in tone, content, pace and style. You'll find writing email a lot easier when you have identified they types of emails you want to send. Bookmark this page: you're going to want to come back here!

The clever guys over at Digital Marketer have identified three types of emails that we can use to communicate with customers, and each type of email has its distinct uses.

First we have what are called **transactional emails** - these are things like appointment confirmations, pre-visit appointment reminders, sales receipts or password reminders. The beauty of this type of email is that it's the one the customer is *most* happy to receive: for example I wouldn't unsubscribe from a mailing list for my dentist for sending an appointment reminder for next Tuesday.

The very astute reader will quickly realise that there is an opportunity here: you can piggy-back a transactional email with something else. This is becoming much more widespread in email marketing now. A very common example is the bottom paragraph of Amazon sales receipts: "Customers Who Bought" is piggy-backing a promotional message on the back of a transactional email. They are encouraging extra spend in an email you don't mind receiving.

Then we have **relational** emails: these are your salon newsletters or blog articles - the emails where you're just delivering great information. You don't get a lot of direct sales for this kind of email, but they are great for communicating your brand, building the trust between you and your customer, keeping you present in the customer's mind and adding important value (i.e. if you are sharing great tips on summer haircare that your customer finds useful, they are unlikely to unsubscribe today).

Lots of marketers forget about this kind of communication and it is a real mistake. It isn't just true of email marketing either: your social media message needs some relational content too. For a really in-depth look at this, check out Gary Vaynerchuk's *Jab, Jab, Jab, Right Hook*[3].

Finally we have **promotional** emails: this is where we send offers, free trials or sale announcements to our customers in an effort to steer them towards profitable products and services, increase frequency of visit, re-engage lost customers, reward loyalty, etc.

These tend to be the easiest emails to write and also the ones most salon owners seem fearful of sending, which is unfortunate. Maybe I've been lucky, but the feedback I get

---

[3] Vaynerchuk, G. *Jab,Jab,Jab, Right Hook*, Harper Business 2013

from my customers about my promotional emails is very positive and I love putting a great campaign together and watching the appointment book fill up as a result.

The most important thing is that you understand how vital it is that you send a *mix* of these types of emails.  If you are only sending transactional emails you are missing out on a vast amount of marketing potential.  Essentially you have the systems in place but you're not working the system to help you achieve your business goals.

Too much relational content means you're not turning your hard work into sales.  Your customers may love receiving your hints and tips and salon news, but let's not forget we're supposed to be engaging in profitable activity here.  Transactional emails are great for building and maintaining loyalty but that's a slow burn before it translates to extra profits for you.

Too much promotional content will tire your audience very quickly.  If the only message they get from you is "buy, buy, buy" you'll suffer on two fronts: either

a)  the customers love the promotions, take you up on all of them and stop paying full price for anything: you are training them to not book ahead and always wait for the next promotion to come along, or

b)  the customers don't like the promotions and unsubscribe

Every salon has it's own ideal "mix" of emails, with the mix depending heavily on the other marketing you're currently doing, the attitude of your customers to email and their demographic. In my own salon, as you will see, I send a strong promotion out every three months. More than that hurts my profitability and less than that makes me feel I'm spending too much time writing emails that aren't translating into sales.

For now, put the "mix" to one side, and as soon as you have a clear understanding of the types of emails you can send and the goals you can strive for through email marketing, we can make a start on sending your first emails. No excuses, we're going to start sending emails today! I know there is a lot more to learn, I know there's a whole section on understanding your database coming but I think it's important for you to enjoy some easy wins early on in the process. The sooner I can share with you how easy email marketing is, the better. Also we're going to have a little brainstorming exercise first and I think it's useful to have a few ideas for emails in mind while we are talking about email marketing.

On the next page is a worksheet called **transactional emails**. There is a special worksheet pack which you can download from hairybooks.com/email which makes all of the worksheets in this book available to you free.

## Transactional Email Worksheet

First, set up your email service or familiarise yourself with your reception system email module

List ALL of the emails you are currently sending, then mark them (T) for Transactional, (R) for Relational and (P) for Promotional. List them and write the frequency you are sending too.

## Transactional Email Worksheet

Brainstorm all of the TRANSACTIONAL emails you COULD be sending in your salon business.

Which ONE of these are you going to work on first?

What is the TRIGGER?

What is the OFFER?

Now go ahead and send it out! You'll want to revisit this email when you have completed the rest of the book, but for now GET IN THE GAME!

There are a couple of reasons we're starting with transactional emails.  Firstly, they tend to be the easiest to get started on and the sooner you're sending emails the happier I am!  More importantly though, transactional emails are very often neglected as part of an email marketing strategy and they're easy to write too.  This is a shame because they are the emails customers most *want* to receive.

For example, let's say I ordered a new iPad on Amazon today.  Do you think the emails I get from Amazon in the next few days are invasive?  Or unnecessary?  Will I ignore them?  Or unsubscribe?  NO WAY!  I'll be checking the confirmation carefully, I'll be opening every email about dispatch and delivery and with my last Amazon purchase I even got a promotional credit the day after delivery too.

Transactional emails are welcome news to our customers and you need to maximise on their excitement and enthusiasm

So let's turn to our worksheets.  Step one is to either sign up and familiarise yourself with an email service, or brush up your learning for the email module of your reception system. I know it's a little box but there's big learning in there!

In the next box I've left some space for you to have a bit of a brainstorm. In this section I want you to list all of the emails you *currently* send your customers. I know for some of you that might be a very short list indeed and that's okay. We all started with a blank page at some stage!

Once you've made your list mark each email with a T for transactional, R for relational or P for promotional, and next to each email write the frequency with which you're sending the email out.

In box number three I want you to brainstorm all the **transactional** emails you *could* send. Let me give you a couple of examples to get you going:

- An email to confirm when a customer books an appointment. Even if you are sending SMS appointment reminders you could also be sending email reminders a day or two before someone visits.

- You could email all your new customers after their first visit with a satisfaction survey.

- You might consider emailing your customers on the anniversary of their first visit with you.

- What about a special email on their birthday?

- We might want to send an email following a specific service: for example in my salon and we send an after-care email when someone has had a set of hair extensions.

Make a list of all transactional emails you *could* be sending. Don't edit the list at all, this is just time for a brain dump. I think you could probably come up with at least 10 ideas without breaking into a sweat.

The reason this exercise is important is it will show you the kind of emails you could send but more importantly it will give you a clear indication of the *kind of information* you will need to start collecting from your customers. Suddenly there is much more to email than just a list of email addresses: to tick off all of the emails on your list you'll need some personal details from your customers and some information about their relationship with your salon too.

Next I want you to select just *one* of the emails you've identified that you'd like to start working on straightaway. If you have a reception system you could probably choose pretty much anything, though of course a lot will depend on the details you have for your customers. For example, there's no point in working on a promotion to send out a birthday promotion if you haven't been collecting the dates from your customers. If you're working from an email service you might be a little more limited as your data export will quickly become out of date with appointment details.

Next, you need to clarify the trigger for that transactional email: what has to happen or what does the customer have to do (or indeed *not* do) in order for your email to be sent to them?

In the next box write down what your offer is going to be - yes we're going to be including an offer. I know this is a transactional email, but we're going to piggy-back a promotion in there too. "Offer" doesn't necessarily mean a discount (though it could if you wanted it too), but we want to include something to encourage some extra *spend*. Are you going to give a voucher for someone's birthday? Or could you offer an additional add-on service to chase a little upgrade spend? Or perhaps you want to tell customers about an after-care product relating to a certain service.

It's time to get this email set up and ready to send. At this stage I don't actually care if you have no email addresses to send out to yet: we're coming to address collection (or 'building our lists') in a later chapter. What is important right now is that you are familiar with *how* to do this, and I want your first transactional email set up and running in the background.

The great thing about transactional emails is they don't need to be particularly creative or clever. You will probably want to re-visit this email after you've learnt a little more about writing copy and coming up with subject lines. For now though keep things really simple. I'm not expecting anything more inventive as a subject line for an appointment reminder than "Your appointment with Bravo on Tuesday", for example. Right now the important thing is to just get in the game and start getting past some of those fears you may hold over speaking to your customers through email. You communicate with your customers every day: all we're doing is changing how they receive some of those messages.

"If I asked you how would you talk to a customer you wouldn't have much of a problem figuring that out, but the second I put technology between you and the customer, things get foggy".

*Chris Davis, ActiveCampaign*

How are you feeling about sending emails now that you're sending? I'm hoping you're at least a *little* less daunted by the prospect and starting to see the potential for this very versatile marketing pillar in your salon business.

With your new sense of triumph, let's take a closer look at your database. Relax. It's less techy than it sounds.

# PART TWO

## Understanding your Database

## Your database

At its most basic, an email database is simply a list of email addresses. That will get you so far and there are indeed some occasions when you'll want to email your whole database (relational emails, for example, can sometimes be sent to everyone at once), but we've already touched on the fact that this may not be enough for an effective marketing campaign. There is a very basic rule of marketing which applies here: the more accurately you can identify a customer or potential customer and tailor your message to her, the more likely she is to respond positively to your email.

That means for your salon promotional activity you'll find the customer response increases greatly when you break your list down into smaller chunks so that you can tailor your news, offers and information to a smaller group.

By way of example, compare these two emails:

- For email one, we going to promote a new nail colour to a random list of 100 people.

The problem is many of the recipients will be uninterested in your marketing message. Broadly speaking, most men on your randomly generated list may not be interested, people who have just had their nail service carried out in the last couple of days will probably ignore your email, clients who are only interested in coming to your salon for waxing services will probably ignore your email and customers who live too far away to travel to your salon will be uninterested too.

- For email two, we'll send the same promotion to a list of 100 female customers who had gel nails 2 to 3 weeks ago, who live within 5 miles of your salon and who do not have an appointment currently booked

Which email do you think will have the best result and make the most impact on its audience? Of course, the second one will generate a lot more potential spend and generally it is because the audience has been more tightly defined.

However, we can only tailor our messages if we are recording the relevant information, or *data*, so our list of email addresses in this case is much more powerful if the customer record also showed:

- The date of the customer's last service
- The customer's gender
- A list of services they have had in the past
- The customer's ZIP code or postcode

Each piece of information on a database record is saved in a **field** and we use these fields to identify groups of customers. One field would be the last service a customer has had, one for her postcode, and so on.

Of course, the best response you can hope for would be to individually email each customer with something tailored specifically for her as an individual, but that isn't terribly realistic as we scale our efforts. Breaking your database into defined chunks is the best we can hope for on a regular basis. Dividing a database in this way is called **segmentation:** think of the segments of an orange. We are identifying a slice of your database and tailoring our marketing as best we can to that segment

In big business, companies who take email marketing seriously and who have lots of resources and time available can run very targeted campaigns like this all the time. If you can find the time to do it in the salon please do, at least occasionally. However I have written this book for the busy owner/manager who is looking to get in the game with email, so for our month-in and month-out purposes we need to be practical. In an effort to save some time (and make the task perhaps a little less daunting) I'll show you how I divide my own list into four much broader categories where we can use email marketing to:

- Keep us in the customers mind
- Drive customers towards profitable products and services, and
- Extend the lifespan of customers through reengagement

Once you have a handle on how to run regular campaigns to broader categories of customer you can run much more highly targeted campaigns alongside in the future.

Here's a picture of how I segment my database for my email campaigns:

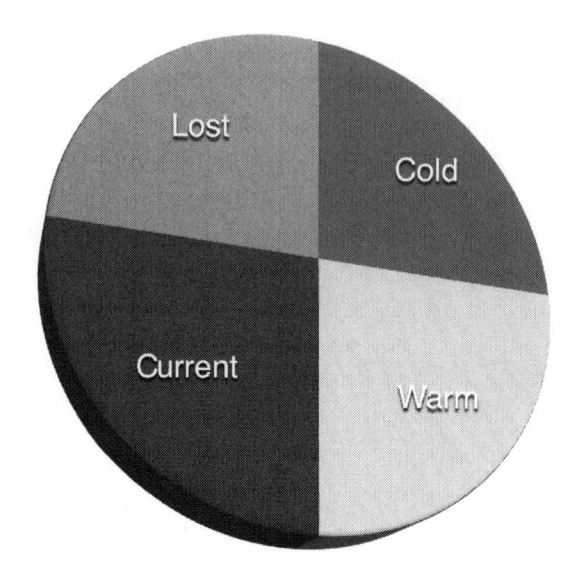

[Pie chart with four segments labeled: Lost, Cold, Warm, Current]

We will be referring to these categories heavily in the coming chapters. My database is divided into cold, warm, current and lost customers and next chapter I will take you through each segment in turn before we look at some ideas of how we can build each segment in our email list.

## Your database, segmented

In my mind, if you have someone's email address they will fall into one of the following four categories.

First we have what's called **cold data**. Cold customers (sometimes called cold prospects) are those people you're able to communicate with through email, but who have never had any dealings with your salon and the potential customer has not had enough information to make any sort of opinion about your products or services yet. Trying to turn a cold prospect into a paying customer is hard work: these people are generally the most resistant to your message and tailoring that message is tough without an existing pattern of spend to draw on, but it is possible to start building that relationship of knowing, liking and trusting in an effort to turn them into your customers in the future.

If cold customers have never heard of us, how are we able to send them emails? Well, in the email marketing business, one main source is by renting or purchasing email mailing lists. There are specialised providers who will walk you through the process and you will get the rights to use a list of contacts, normally for a fixed amount of time.

In our industry I'm afraid I really don't pay any attention to purchasing cold data. It doesn't interest me and I believe that if your salon is supported with your online and social media marketing there is hardly any eventuality when I can imagine buying cold data. I think perhaps the only exception would be if I was opening a new salon in a town where I had no reputation, though to be honest I can think of more effective (and cost-effective) ways of building my email database. It *is* possible to contact cold data without buying or renting lists and in a later chapter I will show you how we can do this in a more ethical and dignified way.

Next, we have your **warm prospects**. These are the people you have email addresses for, they have at least heard of the salon, but they have yet to make a purchase from your business. Some of these appear almost magically on your database of their own accord if you have online bookings. They are people who have registered, booked an appointment and then later cancelled, so they appear on your database but still have yet to make a purchase. You can also build your warm prospects list in various ways, and we'll explore some of those in the next chapter.

Third, we have your **current** customers. We identify those as people who have either made a purchase in the last few weeks or months or who are currently booked in for a future paid-for service.

Then finally we have your **lost** customers. These are people who have spent money in the past, but not for a while and they haven't booked to spend money with you in the future either. How *long* you leave it before a customer is classed as lost is a tricky one and the best place to draw the line varies a lot between salons, but there are some loose guidelines I can share that will help you decide.

The tricky thing is knowing when they are "lost" and when they are "infrequent": we all have those customers who think a once-a-year trim is all they need, or only come for waxing before a vacation.  Unfortunately leaving it a year to class a customer as lost is way too long.  If you have a client visiting a hair salon every eight weeks, she may have been to another salon six times in a year.  If she has been six times it is fairly safe to assume the salon she has been visiting isn't completely useless and so she will have started building loyalty to that salon, which makes getting her back into *your* salon really tough.  The other end of the scale represents a problem too: if you class a customer as lost too soon, say at seven weeks, you may be promoting and trying to bring a customer back in with incentives, offers or discounted services when she may be a lovely loyal client who happens to leave it eight, nine or 10 weeks between haircuts.  That will quickly begin to hurt your profitability and start an undesirable pattern of spend in your customer.

Where you ultimately draw the line really depends on how long your clients tend to leave it between visits.  If your average in a hair salon is, say, six weeks you can probably assume clients are wandering off after about 12 weeks.  If your average is eight weeks you could consider making the cut off later.  I wouldn't go much higher than about 15 or 16 weeks though.  For something like a nail bar where you might expect a visit much more frequently, say a 2.5 week average, you can probably class her as lost much sooner, at around the four week mark.

You will need to monitor and adjust this cut-off point a couple of times a year, and definitely if it feels like you're discounting a lots of visits that would have happened anyway.

Some salon software systems have a pre-defined lost list you can extract from your database with ease. Otherwise, to identify your list of lost customers you will need to:

1. Calculate your average return visit in weeks. This is something I think you should be monitoring as one of your salon Key Performance Indicators anyway. Again, some systems make finding this bit of information really very easy. Contact your system support team for help if you need to.

    Calculating this manually is possible but the calculation is a bit 'rough and ready'. Take the total number of client visits in the year and divide by the number of clients you have. This will show you how many visits on average a customer has with you in 12 months. Divide 52 weeks by *this* number to see your average return visit period in weeks.

2. Now we need a list of customers with email addresses who haven't returned for approximately *double* your average return visits period. Do not just extract the list and send emails blindly to them the first few times: cast your eye over the list and see if there are names you recognise for customers you know are not lost. If there *are* names you know

aren't lost it probably means you have set the criteria a little too low. This is probably one instance where I would err on the side of caution as it is probably better to market to customers who are definitely lost but tougher to get back than it is to class current customers incorrectly.

Before you start marketing to your lost customers you will also need to do just a little staff training. We salon workers are delicate flowers and we don't tend to take rejection terribly well! You *must* make sure that your staff are ready and prepared to welcome lost customers back into the salon and with the right attitude. In my salon we have three rules regarding lost customers: you're more than welcome to copy if you find them useful.

1. We greet the customer like an old friend returning. We welcome them with a smile and genuine warmth. They are back in the salon and prepared to spend money so it's great to see them!

2. We never *ever* criticise the work of others. You don't know what she asked for in the other salon and you don't know what advice she received. Even if the pink and yellow stripes in front of you are hideous, patchy and over-processed, you may *not* pass judgement!

3. Only the salon manager may ask why the customer left us. It is not your employee's job to ask why a customer stopped coming to the salon. The

manager *may* ask, as long as the question is phrased in a way that makes it clear that we want to avoid making the same mistakes again. You don't *have* to ask on the first return visit, or even at all if it feels uncomfortable or embarrassing.

You may find to begin with that you don't have email addresses for your lost customers at all if you haven't been collecting email addresses for a period of time. That's not important: what is important is that you and your staff understand the importance of getting full client details from now on. In my experience, beauty therapists are generally better at getting full details than hairdressers.

Do we leave customers on your lost list forever? There are varying opinions on this. Some feel that you should wait until the lost customer unsubscribes before you remove their details.

> "My view is to continue emailing them until they unsubscribe from the database as that is their choice"
>
> *Neil Prigent, Jas Salons*

The alternative train of thought is that mailing to an unresponsive list flags you as a potential source of spam to the customer's email service and will hurt deliverability of your emails going forward.

> "There is a point of no return … we generally will go out about 4 or 5 months and then stop."
>
> *Bart Foreman, Endgame Marketing Solutions*

Whatever you decide, there are one or two occasions when I think it's *definitely* OK to remove the names.

The first would be if a customer has really caused some trouble in the salon. I had an incident recently where a customer made quite a fuss because she couldn't choose who to have her complimentary blow-dry with. Read that again: her *complimentary* blow-dry. With a big spender or a really loyal client I'd have bent over backwards, but I reviewed our records and realised her last 3 visits had been "troubled" with me having to step in to resolve silly issues. Also, I'd seen her all over Facebook liking and sharing to win a hair colour service with a competitor: there was no loyalty there.

Second, where a customer only EVER comes in when you contact her with a discount as a lost client I'd suggest you can afford to move her off the list. Offer-chasers can be a lot more work than their bill justifies and it's a quick way to demotivate your staff. Don't abandon these clients forever though. A clever idea would be to move her to a new "Fillers" list. You could market to these customers only when you know you have a slow week coming up, or when you have a new starter's column to fill.

Now that you have an understanding of the parts of your database join me in the next chapter where we will work on some ideas to build the number of contacts you have in each segment.

## Growing your Email List

I'm hoping by now you can see the importance of keeping your email list up together and what I find interesting is when I have started a salon owner on the email marketing journey, they very quickly start to look for opportunities to grow their lists in and among the customer care and marketing they are already doing day-to-day.

It's important to have some list-building strategies for each segment tied into your policies and procedures if the long-term impact of your email marketing is to be maintained and enhanced.

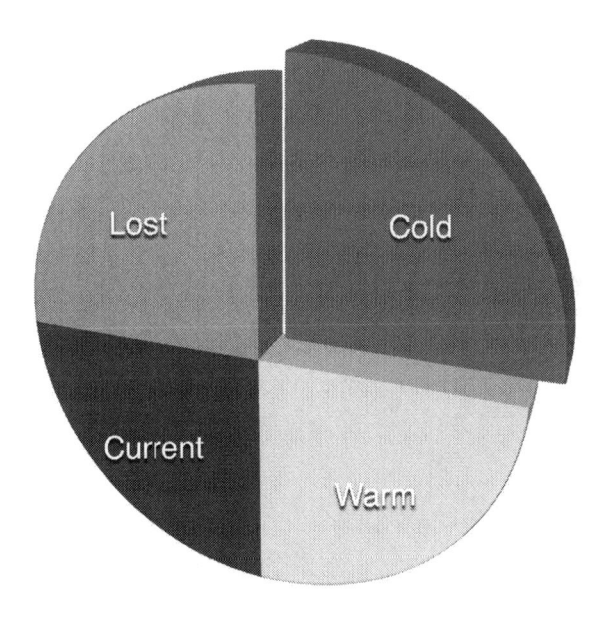

First up we have our cold customers. You'll remember from the last chapter that these are clients who have not heard of our salon and have not formed an opinion about our products or services. I've already said that I don't really like the idea of buying or renting cold data, so how on earth do we build a cold client list?

Well, in short we don't. What I suggest you do instead is make a list of your network contacts who have a list of customers you would like to reach.

Basically, you're trying to find someone who has a similar target market to you but who is not competing. Some partnerships are obvious: for example your hair salon may have a very similar target market to the beauty salon down the road. Some partnerships are a little more subtle and take some extra work. This whole exercise relies heavily on you having a very clear understanding of who your target market is.

A technique very often referred to these days is identifying a **customer avatar**. Essentially this is an exercise in defining a typical desirable customer for your business. I have four in my salon: they are imaginary people with a set of characteristics that make up my target market. The most important in my salon is called Jenny. I know an awful lot about her. I know that Jenny has two children of university age (one is Lisa, who happens to be salon avatar number two), she works in a professional capacity for a large local firm and can work from home a day or two per week. I know the street she lives in, that she is on her second marriage (to Rob, salon avatar number three). I know where she likes to go on holiday and even what she listens to in the car. I know what she worries about and what keeps her awake at night. I know what she earns and most importantly what I can offer her as a customer. You can either build your own Jenny by surveying your current customers or, if you are looking to shift your customer base, your Jenny would be your *ideal* customer.

Now it's a case of identifying who might have a list of "Jenny"s in your area. What are Jenny's hobbies? Are there any groups or classes she is a member of? Where else does she shop? What is her favourite coffee shop, bar or restaurant? Now go through your professional network and identify two or three partners who may be able to help you.

What you *can't* do is simply roll up and ask for their list of emails. Indeed you can get into all sorts of legal problems by sending emails to someone who did not sign up to receive them from you. What you *can* do is work with your promotional partner and ask them to contact their list on your behalf, usually as part of a reciprocal arrangement.

In my experience, there is right way and a wrong way to approach this. The wrong way is to contact your prospective promotional partner and directly ask them to market to their list on your behalf. What will usually work better is if, in the first instance, you volunteer to contact *your* list with a promotional message from the potential partner. Following on from that, you could say "Hey, my customers really enjoyed reading your content and I was wondering whether your customers would enjoy reading mine too. How about we work together in the future?" Handled properly, this kind of joint promotion is mutually beneficial and terrific for customers too.

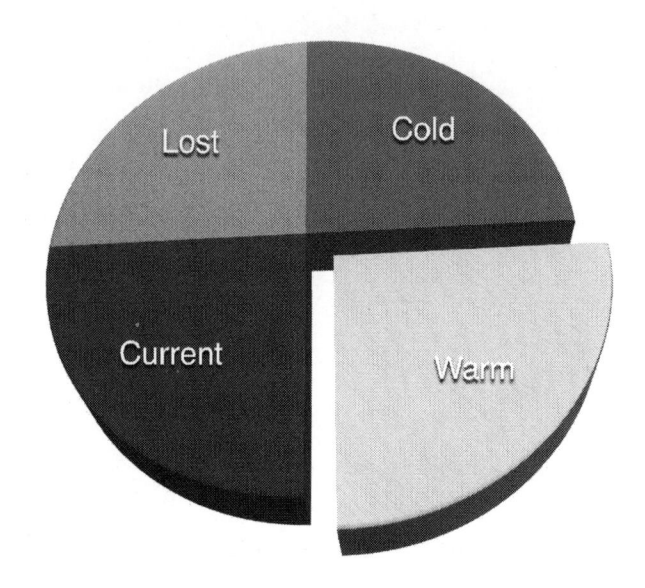

Now let's turn to your warm prospects. If you remember, these guys have heard of us but they are still at the "checking us out" stage and have yet to commit to spending booking or spending any money in our salon.

So why is it important to build your warm prospects list? And where do they come from? Well, it's important because these are your *future* customers. They are essential for your continued growth and the bigger we can build your warm client list and the quicker we can persuade them to become current clients, the more rapid your potential growth. The trick is to make sure your list of warm clients is a good one: it's not enough to build a massive list if they are a bad fit for your salon and what you offer, so keep referring to your customer avatar.

It is unusual for people to take a blind jump into a purchasing decision with a salon. Either online or offline, they ask around, do some research, check your salon ratings and reviews, get to know your brand a little. Asking customers to jump straight from your cold list into your current list is a bit like asking a blind date to marry you: it's ineffective at best and a little bit creepy too.

Your warm list, however, have heard of you and may have been thinking of coming in for a while. So how can we build our list?

As I've mentioned, some names seem to appear on your list as if by magic. If you have online bookings as part of your computerised reception system, some potential customers may have booked an appointment online and then cancelled before coming in, so they appear on your list without having made a purchase.

You can also successfully build your warm prospects list through social media. For example, I successfully use Facebook contests and giveaways to grow my warm prospects email list. Unfortunately Facebook doesn't currently allow you to just scrape email addresses from your online followers, but there are some nifty online options which can help.  Once you get the hang of this, you'll never want to do a "like and share" contest again, I promise!

You can further build your warm list through your offline competitions and ads.  For example, you might decide it's appropriate for you to run a competition in your local newspaper (because Jenny reads it).  Instead of entrants posting their entry, you could require them to enter online in an effort to build your mailing list.  It's now a requirement of all our offline promotions that we get emails for our warm list as part of the exercise: if we can't get the emails we don't take part in the promotion.

Speak to your friendly web designer about including a signup form on your website.  Realistically you probably will not get very many signups this way, but the cost is minimal and the lead tends to be a very good one if they have already visited your website and want to know more.  It won't revolutionise your marketing but it's a source of leads that is often overlooked on salon websites.

More ambitious list-builders might consider creating a **lead magnet**.  This sounds very technical but you see will have seen these online all the time.  They are accompanied by a signup form and usually will be something like "7 ways to add volume to your hair without backcombing".  The warm lead swaps their email address for the great information you're providing, usually delivered as a short video or a downloadable PDF.  Lead magnets can be advertised from your website or, in our industry, really successfully on social media.  You will either need the help of your web designer to put together a signup page (often called a **squeeze page**) or you can cut out the need for a page by using Facebook's Lead Ads: your warm lead signs up for your lead magnet on the Facebook platform rather than being sent to your website at all.

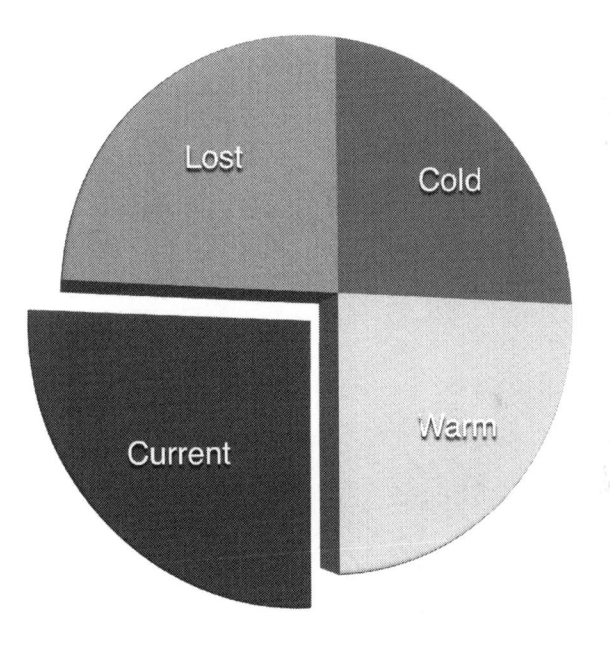

Building your current list is a little more straightforward. Hopefully you already have consultation forms or client information forms in the salon and ready to use.  Check that they are being used consistently by your team and that there is space for customers email.

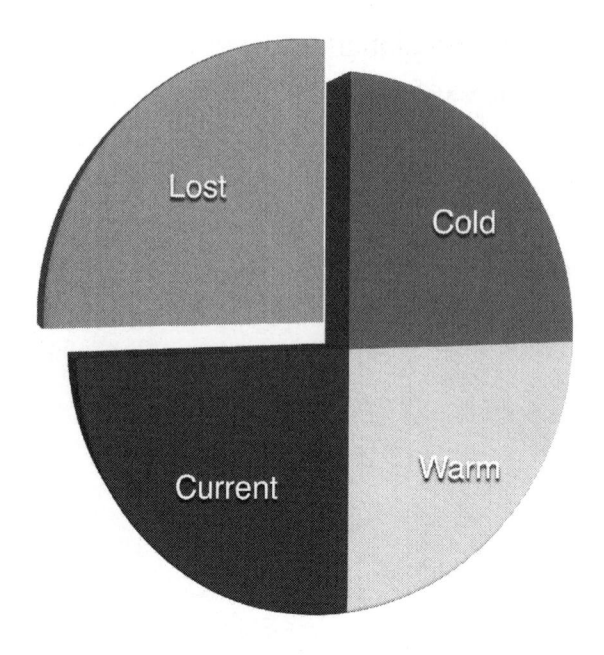

"Collecting email addresses is one of the most valuable things you can do, it's an essential part of not only retaining loyal clients but also building a new client base".

*Alex Quinn, Phorest*

It's really important that you communicate the importance of getting these forms filled out your staff. They need to understand that it supports an important marketing pillar in your business. Make collecting this information routine and part of your salon policies and procedures.

Building your current list is absolutely vital because it is also the only way of getting details for our lost customers. There is, unfortunately, no dignified way of going back to get lost customers' details after they have lapsed. The only way to populate your future lost customer list is by ensuring your current list is up-to-date now.

Once you have a process in place for building your current list, build into your policies and procedures a system for getting details updated.

> "Data should be as clean and accurate as possible."
>
> *Jo Burgess, Shortcuts*

Perhaps once a year you could get to your current customers to confirm their details are up to date: we do this every January. Also it is useful to train your staff to recognise cues for when an updated form may be needed. For example if one of your current customers is talking about changing her job, her email address might be changing too.

Now that we have a good understanding of your database and some ideas for how you could be building your list in each segment, let's start putting together a schedule for sending emails to each segment.

## Your Sending Schedule

Now that we have an understanding of your database and how to build your list, in this chapter were going to start compiling a schedule of emails to send to each segment of your database. We're going to build a calendar you can work towards over the coming days and weeks.

It's really important to me that you start seeing progress and results as soon as possible, so please don't wait until you have your list built in every segment. If all you have is a small part of your current database to work with, get started on that and build your lists while you are marketing.

There is an email planning worksheet in the download section of hairybooks.com/email or one on the following page for you to copy. The planning worksheet covers three-months of emails, then I simply cycle through the plan four times each year.

The first thing we can add to the planning worksheet is our transactional emails. If you remember, these are the lovely "set-up and send" emails that tick over in the background with very little interference from us. Don't ignore the importance of these emails: they are an easy win in marketing terms and can have powerful results.

Next we will start planning our cold data activity. Before we start planning *any* email activity it's important to revisit what is is we're hoping to achieve. That puts a firm perspective on our results when we are reviewing at the end of each

|  | Cold | Warm | Current | Lost |
|---|---|---|---|---|
| Month 1 | Ideally twice a month | Here's some great info | Here's some info plus an offer | Here's an AMAZING offer |
| Month 2 | Ideally twice a month | Here's some info plus an offer | Here's an AMAZING offer | Here's some great info |
| Month 3 | Ideally twice a month | Here's an AMAZING offer | Here's some great info | Here's some info plus an offer |

Transactional Emails

month. As far as our cold data is concerned, all we really want them to do is to begin the process of warming up. Essentially we are trying to get our cold prospect to know, like and trust us enough to move on to the warm list.

So how exactly do we do that? Well, what we **don't** do is continually try to sell: so in month one, all we are going to provide is some great information. For example, imagine our fictitious beauty salon is writing some great information to send to hair clients. You could write a really useful piece about summer skincare and ask the hair salon to send on your behalf. You could include an offer, or even just ask them to contact you or go to your website for more information. This is not an opportunity for hard sell. In the other direction, the hair salon could come up with some brilliant party hair tips in time for Christmas and ask the beauty salon to send those out.

In months two and three we're just going to send more information: remember we may not even have email addresses for this part of our audience yet. If the relationship moves on, if they ask for more information or opt in to your mailing list (and you should give them the opportunity to do both on every email), the prospect comes into your warm list and we treat them slightly differently. Until that time, all were going to do is deliver great information.

With your warm list, the goal is to warm them up enough to finally make a booking or purchase. We've already established with our cold data that a great way to build trust with a potential customer is to deliver excellent information: so you can see in month one we're going to do exactly that. It might be the *same* information you giving your cold data as long as it is appropriate. At this stage I hope you can begin to put to one side any concerns you may have about email marketing being a continual, invasive hard sell. In fact we have scheduled four months of emails and haven't even tried to sell anything at all yet!

In month two for our warm prospects we're going to add in an offer. This is not going to be a massive discount, it is not a loss-leader, but something much more gentle. Maybe an upsell offer or a discount on a product purchased with a full-price service. We are trying to position our salon in the prospect's mind and give them a realistic expectation of what they can expect going forward as a customer. Receiving a massive discount every month is *not* what they can expect but the occasional upsell won't do our brand any harm and might be just the excuse your potential customer is looking for to make a booking.

Then in month three we are going to send an amazing offer: something that will really grab their attention and persuade them to spend right now. We are not offering massive discounts every month which runs the risk of cheapening the brand. We are also avoiding the difficulty that continual promotional discounts bring in trying to create urgency: we want to be able to direct larger numbers of new customers to the months when you want them to visit.

Now let's turn to our current customers. I suspect this pattern is going to start looking very familiar very soon!

In month one we send appropriate upsell offer. You can't really copy and paste your offer from your warm customers as your relationship with them is at a different stage: these are people that are already spending your salon so it's important that we look to maximising profitability rather than harming it. An appropriate offer might be a discount on a product purchased with a full-priced service, or a discounted additional service.

In month 2 our current customers will receive an amazing offer of their own. This again will have to be slightly different to your warm prospects as we are marketing to existing customers. You can still afford to be really generous as long as you are targeting them with a service which is new to the salon, or with a service which is new to that particular customer, or with products they haven't tried before. I have also worked with salons who have successfully run a gift card sale for their current customers and I would include a generous recommend-a-friend scheme in this category too.

Finally for current customers in month three they will receive some great information. Here it is quite acceptable to minimise your work by repurposing the information emails from another segment.

Finally let's turn to our lost customers. It's only fair to warn you that this is the segment of the database I hit the hardest of all with discounts.  It's also only fair to point out that I get a large amount of criticism for that from other salon coaches over this (and in fact over most of my opinions!) but I am a firm believer in what is called the **price/ experience match**[4].  Essentially the theory runs that most people stop coming to your salon *not* because they hate you, *not* because you did a particularly horrible job, but because they didn't feel you were offering good value for money any more.  By reducing the price through an offer or discount to a level that matches (or is below) their perceived experience, we are occasionally given a chance to get them back through the salon door and given the opportunity to impress them once again.  My advice is to *be bold* with your lost customer discounts and bear in mind that they won't have the opportunity to take advantage of those discounts month after month: if we manage to get them back through the door they land back on your current customer list and won't receive the same generous discounts again.  I *would* say however that you should monitor recurring lost customers.  If people end up on this list you may have set the threshold for lost too low, or you may just have a little sneak who has figured out your system and is manipulating it to receive offers.

In month 2, our lost customers get an information email and once again you could re-purpose the email from your Cold prospects, and then in month 3 our lost customers receive a

---

[4] For more on this see Austin-Smith, A, *The Fantastic Hairdresser*, Fantastic Hairdresser Company Ltd. 2003

more gentle upsell offer, similar to our warm and current customers.

You might decide to do the same emails across-the-board: for example all categories receive information in month one, an upsell offer in month two and a heavy discount in month three. I'm not a fan of this as it can feel a bit like everybody on your list is getting a big discount in the same month. This can be demotivating, particularly if you have an employed team, but if your list is currently small I can see the appeal and advantages.

That looks like quite a full calendar doesn't it? Well there is actually a fair bit more work to do here I'm afraid, because we don't just send *one* email per month to each segment. Join me in the next chapter where we will look at the planning of your email campaigns.

## Planning your Campaigns

Now that we have an idea about the type of email with going to send, let's look specifically at when we are going to send each email as part of a well thought-out campaign.

Going back to your email planner, the reality is that with your cold prospects the sending of the emails is probably not up to you.  The timing and frequency will be set by the person who owns the list and they will probably make you work around any email activity they already have planned for themselves.  Ideally you would want to contact your cold prospects a couple of times every month: realistically take what you're offered with a smile!  Anything is better than nothing even if that is only one send as an isolated campaign.

For the rest of the calendar my scheduling would look something like this:

**For information emails**

- I would send the first email on or around the first of the month
- I would send a follow-up email on or around the 15th

For example if I was a hair salon, I might send three chic party hair ideas I had spotted on celebrities on 1 December, then on the 15th I might send some pictures of salon work on the same theme.

|  | Cold | Warm | Current | Lost |
|---|---|---|---|---|
| Month 1 | Ideally twice a month | 1st Month<br>15th Month | 1st Month<br>8th Month | 1st Month<br>Resend to non-openers<br>Summary 8th<br>Final reminder 17th |
| Month 2 | Ideally twice a month | 1st Month<br>8th Month | 1st Month<br>Resend to non-openers<br>Summary 8th<br>Final reminder 17th | 1st Month<br>15th Month |
| Month 3 | Ideally twice a month | 1st Month<br>Resend to non-openers<br>Summary 8th<br>Final reminder 17th | 1st Month<br>15th Month | 1st Month<br>8th Month |

**Transactional Emails**

**For an upgrade offer**

- Again I would send the first email on or around the first of the month

- I would send a second email ONLY to people who have not responded to the upgrade offer around a week later on the eighth

**For an amazing jaw-dropping offer**

- For the lucky customers getting the amazing offer this month I would send the first email on the first of the month

- It is completely acceptable to resend the same email four or five days later *only* to people who did not open the first email: you don't have to change anything. Most reception systems sadly fail at this point as they aren't sophisticated enough to send to non-openers. This is why I use ActiveCampaign for my promotional emails as services like this handle automation with ease

- I would email a short reminder of the promotion around the eighth of the month

- Then I would send a third and final email about five days before the promotion closes. I like my promotions to be finished by the end of week three so I would be sending my last email on or around the 17th of the month

There are a couple of **rules** which help with your scheduling. The first is that we *never* schedule an email for a day when the salon is closed. Even if you're asking customers to click a link or reply to your email, most months at least one person will pick up the phone. Don't miss that opportunity by sending your email on a day that the salon isn't open.

Rule number two is you never schedule emails before you've spoken to your staff. Make sure they completely understand what it is that you're sending so that they can answer telephone queries or face-to-face.

Rule number three is to try and hit a sending "hotspot". There are three hotspots per day for my salon.

- The first is between a customer waking and them starting their work day, so usually somewhere between 7:30am and 9am

- The second hotspot hits around lunchtime

- The last hits as my customer ends their day, so after 7pm

Keep your avatar in mind when you are scheduling your emails: for example, if you want your customer's full attention but your avatar has three children to get school, sending before 9:00 in the morning is probably not a smart time.

Experiment with your sending schedule and go with the results even if they fly in the face of common sense and your gut instinct. If you are using an email service many providers learn the best time for sending to your particular list and can make recommendations based on the times your customers are opening their emails: again most salon software systems are unable to do this.

I know that if you haven't sent any emails before that looks like an awful lot of sending. Maybe you're thinking that your customers are going to complain or hit 'unsubscribe' in response to your campaign. Some will. It's a reality of email. In the next chapter we're going to talk all about unsubscribes and get *that* horrible topic out of the way.

## A Word on Unsubscribes

This is the lesson I send my mentoring clients back to again and again. We're going to talk all about unsubscribes.

It would be lovely if, having spent all that time building our lists, our segmented audience was grateful enough to remain loyal, actively search for and open every email we send and click every link we provide. Unsurprisingly, email life just isn't like that.

There are a huge number of reasons why somebody might choose to unsubscribe:

- Maybe your client doesn't think your emails are interesting

- Maybe she thinks you sent too many emails (which is kind of the same thing, really)

- Maybe she has made up her mind not to return to the salon

I will, however, bet you a shiny £1 coin but it does not mean she hates you and wishes you were dead! Yet this is the gravity with which salon owners seem to treat unsubscribes. It's completely irrational and what's worse is they let the unrealistic fear of unsubscribes prevent them from emailing at all.

I'm a curious sort of fellow, so I asked one of my long-term, regular clients why she had unsubscribed from my email list. This is someone who had been coming to the salon for over 10 years and she's a smart lady. You know the sort: she has a good business head on her shoulders and I've respected her opinion on lots of aspects of my business over the years. The reason she gave? She told me she just gets too many emails. That's it! She's a loyal client *to this day* a couple of years after she unsubscribed. The *real* reason people unsubscribe? **You'll never really know,** so stop guessing and making false assumptions.

I must warn you however that if you haven't sent emails to your list before you should be prepared for a small flurry of unsubscribes. It always happens when you start emailing for the first time.

It is important to monitor unsubscribes and in fact it is the second performance measure that I suggest for your email marketing but please do not *obsess* about them. The biggest favour I ever did myself was to turn off the unsubscribe notifications in MailChimp. For years I had to let them send me an email every time someone unsubscribed. How depressing! It's no wonder I was continually anxious!

You need to learn to welcome your unsubscribes: after all, what is the point of an email address for someone who doesn't want to hear from you by email? You really *must* focus on what is left on your list and keep growing your lists. After all, what remains is a group of potential and current customers who are happy to hear from you by email and that is a *truly* valuable resource for your business.

Well done! You've made through the negative chapter, relatively unscathed I hope. In the next chapter we get more positive again. I've mentioned performance measures a couple of times so far: in the next chapter I share with you the measures I monitor in my own businesses.

## Measuring success

We talked about some of the things we want our emails to do: we want to build our list, get the email into the hands of the right people, warm up cold traffic, drive spend and re-engage with lost customers. It's very easy to feel overwhelmed, which I hope I have helped with during the planning process, but it's also difficult to know if you are doing *well*. In this chapter I share with you the measures I am monitoring on a regular basis and I think you should be too in an effort to help you find areas for improvement and so that you can enjoy seeing how your marketing performance is improving.

On the next page is a summary sheet of the measures I use: of course there are lots of things you *could* measure but I find these keep me on an even keel.

The first measure is the **size of your list**, and you will see in the summary that I've broken the list down into the four major segments, cold, warm, current and lost.

It's important to see *growth* in your cold and warm lists, because these are your future customers: this is where your sustained salon growth will be coming from. Don't jump on all signs of growth as improvement though. If you see spikes in the growth of your list but don't see that filtering down into customers you may be growing a list of leads which isn't a good fit with your salon. Keep your customer

# Email KPI Sheet

## 1. Email list size

|  | Count | +/- |
|---|---|---|
| Cold data | _____ | _____ |
| Warm data | _____ | _____ |
| Current clients | _____ | _____ |
| Lost clients | _____ | _____ |

## 2. Unsubscribes

Campaign name: _____

Unsubscribe count: _____

Unsubscribe %: _____

## 3. Open rate

Campaign name: _____

Open %: _____

## 4. Click-through rate

Campaign name: _____

Click-through %: _____

## 5. Revenue generated

Campaign name: _____

Revenue generated: _____

Revenue per open: _____

avatars in mind and speak directly to them in your marketing and emails.

It's great to see growth in your current list, either because the salon is getting busier or because you're filling in gaps in your database which means you can market to more of your current customers.

It seems strange to say that we want to see growth in the number of lost customers: of course we don't want to see a larger number of customers leaving us, but we *do* want to see an increase in the number of customers we are able to reach so that we can try and persuade them back. Monitor the number of lost contacts you have and see if the numbers tally with the number of lost customers your reception system is reporting. Ideally, you want to be able to reach as many of your lost customers as possible.

The second measure is the number of **unsubscribes**. Though I have warned you about the dangers of obsessing about unsubscribes, it's an important measure nonetheless. This is something you will want to measure on a campaign-by-campaign basis. If you see a spike in the number of customers unsubscribing over and above your normal rate you've probably got the tone or content of your emails wrong, or you are frustrating your customers in some way.

> "High opt outs ... are a big warning sign - you are likely to be targeting the wrong people with

the wrong messages, and should review your marketing strategy accordingly."

*Jo Burgess, Shortcuts*

Dig a little deeper and try and find the reasons why *before* your send any more emails.

The third measure is the number of email **opens**: how many of the emails you've sent actually get opened and read. This tells you how good the subject line of your email was and whether you're hitting the customers at the right day or time of their interest.

> "Having collected 1000 email addresses only 200-300 people will read it and this is disappointing, though you should still do it!"

*Neil Prigent, Jas Salons*

I'm afraid many salon reception systems ignore this important measure in their reporting.

Next we want to measure the **click-through-rate**. This is the number of people who took the action you wanted them to as a result of your email. We'll talk about 'calls to action' later on, but if you're asking your customer to call you or take some other action offline, you might want to call this your Response Rate instead.

The final measure of your email success is the **revenue** the emails are generating. I measure this as an average revenue-per-open: that tells you how good your email is once it's been opened. Again, you'll want to monitor this on a campaign by campaign basis.

> "You measure the success by sales: that's it. Anything with the word 'marketing' attached to it, it should be held up to a microscope of 'are you generating revenue?'"
>
> *Chris Davis, ActiveCampaign*

Speak to your salon reception system provider about how to obtain these measures: your list growth should be monitored at least once a month, the other measures on a campaign by campaign basis.

Unfortunately, this is where lots of systems fail, and I find I can get much better information by using a separate email service. As I have already said though, the more of us that raise our voices to our software providers, the quicker they will realise how we're being let down and perhaps bring changes in future versions.

I think it's probably time we got some copywriting under our belts, so join me in the next chapter when we'll get into the real nuts and bolts of our emails and I'll show you how I put my own salon marketing emails together.

## Layout, format and tone

Getting the layout and tone of your email right can be the difference between a campaign catching fire and giving great returns and one fizzling out and getting no traction at all.

Take a look at these two examples from my own Inbox - I'm going to compare two very different styles of email and explore which I think is more appropriate for your salon communications

Let's start with this one[5]: it's a newsletter from the Thames Valley Chamber of Commerce and it came with a big logo header and even a menu on the side.

I don't know the stage of growth an organisation needs to get to before you can forget that real people are reading your emails, but I can state with some certainty that this is *not* what we should be striving for. Lots of salons I have worked with try and emulate bigger organisations by producing this kind of email and it's a *big* mistake. This kind of thing might work for business-to-business organisations but it's rarely tempting for your current and potential customers.

The shame of it is, there's probably been some good money spent on this email and it could be performing much

---

[5] Reproduced by kind permission of Thames Valley Chamber of Commerce. Though I doubt they'll be so keen next time I ask!

### In the Spotlight

**International Trade Training**

When trading internationally you can often experience barriers not encountered when dealing with companies in the UK.

To help businesses overcome this the Chamber runs a full programme of training courses, covering the essential aspects of international trade.

For a list of topics and forthcoming dates click here

In-company training is also available, which can be tailored to your business requirements and delivered at a location of your choice.

Chamber members receive a 25% discount on all TVCC run courses.

better. In my experience working with some really very large B2B concerns I am convinced this sort of email can be counter-productive in lots of cases. My rule of thumb is that businesses don't read emails: *people* do. Talk to people and build a relationship with them!

Compare it to this email[6] from Tracey Miller, who runs Bigger, Brighter, Bolder, another business group which happens to be based locally to me.

I'm a previous member of both Tracey's group and the Chamber of Commerce so I suppose I fall into the same segment of both databases.

---

Hi Phil

As promised here is the booking form for the BBB Empowerment and Firewalk event.

Click here

Don't forget your friends, family and team members.

Tickets are £127. **Use the code BBBmemberLOVE to get your places for £87.**

You're going to love this!

Book early as we only have limited spaces for the event.

Tracey x

BBB SUCCESS GROUPS
*Developing the Mindset for Success*

---

There are some glaring differences, yet both are from local business groups, both trying to sell me on a training event,

---

[6] Reproduced by kind permission of Tracey Miller, Bigger Brighter Bolder.

but what Tracey knows is that to get me to read and respond to her email it's a really good idea to make the email *look like one I want to read.* She has a clear idea about her audience and the email is really well targeted as part of a sequence. I don't even know why I'm receiving the Chamber of Commerce email: I'm a salon owner, an author and a speaker so heaven only knows how I've ended up on the International Trade mailing list. It doesn't speak to me, at least in a tone I respond to and the email looks impersonal. Tracey's email is so friendly, so authentic that she could easily be talking to me personally rather than through a mailing list: in fact I had to really scratch my head to figure out if this was a mailing-list email at all.

Think about the emails you receive. The latest statistic I heard was that we receive an average of over 130 every day. Now, which are the ones that *you* want to read? They're the ones from your friends, your family and your close colleagues. Are they heavily formatted? Full of graphics and headlines?

Of course not! They're short, to the point, pretty plain to look at and what's essential these days is that they load really quickly on a mobile device.

> "An email is not a web page: you do not need to put big images or too many images. Every piece of media you add to an email is going to increase

the chances that it's marked as spam, it's just what it is. Text base emails perform the best."

*Chris Davis, ActiveCampaign*

If you're sending a big, glossy, highly-formatted newsletter-style email and getting disappointing results, try scaling everything back to basics. If you are really dubious about what I say, try conducting what is called a split-test[7]. Send your glossy newsletter to half your database and your back-to-basics version to the rest and monitor the response. As always, go with the results: you are allowed to completely ignore my advice if the results tell you otherwise!

The same goes for the tone of your emails. They should sound friendly, chatty and very natural.

> "One common mistake I see is people trying to come across as 'professional', which completely dilutes the fact that the hairdressing [and salon] industry is so much fun!"

*Jo Burgess, Shortcuts*

If you struggle to sound casual in written communications and they come across as overly formal, try dictating your emails into your phone and then transcribing them: I had to

---

[7] Again, split-testing is easy on a separate email service and possible but a bit of a chore on most salon reception systems.

do my first three or four months this way and still use transcripts of my videos in place of written blogs.

If you did your homework on defining your customer avatars you'll find this very much easier. Keep a really clear picture in your mind of your chosen avatar then simply write your email directly to them. It helps you pitch the email at an appropriate level and it means you'll be communicating with a consistent voice across your emails and other marketing pillars too.

Bearing the tone of your emails in mind, jump into the next chapter when we will finally put some words on the screen in the subject line.

# The Dark Art of Subject Lines

You could write an entire book on writing great subject lines, but unfortunately I'm convinced you'd be wasting your time, because the most irritating thing about subject lines is that what works *now* won't work so well in a year, and what your audience responds to changes as their relationship with you develops and matures too.

Basically, writing subject lines is a bit like archery, it's just that your target happens to be tied to the tail of a slightly startled squirrel.

The subject line of your email is your sales pitch for the open. Just as a newspaper headline is there to get you to read the article, so an email subject line is there to get you to open and read the email.

> "In order to get your clients to open your marketing emails a compelling and interesting subject line is paramount."
>
> *Alex Quinn, Phorest*

Where most salon owners I have worked with go wrong is they think the subject line needs to be a kind of summary field where you give the entire contents of your email in one sentence. This is not true. The *entire* purpose of the subject line is to get the message opened and nothing more.

In a really cluttered inbox, it's your task to make your email subject line stand out which is tough enough. You'll make it even tougher, though, if you're trying to summarise in 10 words the benefits of your latest facial products.

Standing out used to be a little easier: in fact there was a glorious, golden age of email when you could get a real spike in the number of opens by using someone's name in the subject line.

> "It can be difficult to cut though the clutter in your clients' inbox. You can get around this with a few

clever tactics such as incorporating your clients' names in the subject line, keeping content short and snappy, and of course sending out targeted and timely messages."

*Jo Burgess, Shortcuts*

These days we don't kid ourselves that some poor marketing monkey at Amazon is writing personalised emails to us, but there's still a slight pickup when we use someones name. We are, after all, conditioned to respond to our own names from a very early age. Again, split-test it or just throw an occasional personalised subject line and watch the results. If you *are* going to use someone's name, for heaven's sake make sure it's spelt correctly: if you're unsure about the quality of your list I would leave out all of the personalisation for now.

More recently, you can pick up a couple of percentage points in your open rate by using little icons or emoji in your subject line: I expect this benefit will be pretty short-lived but have fun experimenting with them too.

Also bear in mind that your subject line needs to be between 6 and 10 words in length maximum or it may not all be displayed, particularly on our mobile devices

There are two main types of subject line: blind subject lines and direct subject lines.

**Blind subject lines** are the ones that are designed to intrigue you, where you're not entirely sure what the email is about. They're good fun to use but a bit of a cow to write, if I'm honest. I've had some great results with some of these:

> "What's short, pink and got you teased at school?"

> "David Beckham, Jon Snow and your mother on Facebook"

> "I had a dream about you, <insert name>"

It's OK to be a bit cheeky in your subject lines if that's your style and a little controversy can go a long way too. Your customers will soon let you know if you've crossed a line.

**Direct subject lines** make it really clear what is going to be in the email:

> "New announcement . . ."

> "Save £25 on . . ."

> "Your free voucher is attached"

You could do a lot worse than just identifying one main key benefit for your customers and using that as the subject line for an email. For example, if you are promoting skincare to ladies of a certain age a direct subject line might be "Youthful skin in just two weeks".

Direct subject lines tend to be quite a bit easier to write and it's tempting to use them all the time. My advice is to change things up a bit for your customers and monitor your results carefully.  You don't want your list to get bored with hearing from you.  If that means dropping a few blind subject lines into the mix now and again then go for it.

So how do we know if a subject line is performing? Well, our third performance measure for email marketing is called the **open rate** which is the percentage of the emails that you sent that got opened and read.  You're going to be comparing this against the other campaigns that you send, and after a while against the average open rate for your list.  To give you some idea (and this is a *really* rough idea) the industry average open rate is between 20 and 25% depending on who you ask.  This feels really low and is one of the reasons we never send just one email in isolation: they're nearly always sent as part of a two or three part campaign to catch more clients.

> "In the hair and beauty industry we are very lucky to be able to achieve open rates of around 30% for personalised, targeted and timely emails.  Not all industries have this luxury ..."
>
> *Jo Burgess, Shortcuts*

The best open rate I've managed is 85.7% which was awesome.  Usually I can hit between 30 and 60% but I had really bad days too.  My worst ever was 8% which made me feel terrific as you can imagine.  After a while you see open rate as a really important measure and almost more important than your unsubscribe rate. In short, measure your open rate but benchmark *against yourself* and as long as your results are improving over time, which they will if you learn from the lessons of your past campaigns, you should not worry too much about what the rest of the world is achieving.

Some people will tell you to write the rest of your email first then come back to the subject line, some copywriters do the opposite. Personally I like having the subject line finished first. Occasionally I will write the other way round, but if I have a really good subject line in position I find it inspires and spurs me on. Experiment a little and find what works for you, but whatever you do spend a good amount of time on your subject lines - Rule number 1 here is that between 25 and 50% of your total copywriting time should be spent crafting your subject line. Yes, I literally do spend 50% of my writing time on that one little subject line!

Rule number 2 is to *never* waste a good subject line on a poor email. I'm sure you're shocked and would never want to send an email that isn't incredible and filled with wit, personable humour and superb information but you are human. The calendar is king in my business and if you know you have until 11am to send a campaign, it's 10:40am and you're still not ready there may be times when an email goes out that you're not totally ecstatic about *and that's fine* as long as it won't actually harm your business by sending it. However you should never waste a terrific subject line on a mediocre email. Save it until the muse returns.

Which brings me to rule 3 and the first thing I want you to do when you finish this chapter. You *must* put together a file for your headlines. You will want to record all the subject lines you use in your emails, especially those that do particularly well. This way you always have inspiration to hand. Add to the file any email subject lines from other people that catch your eye. Don't just grab it and send, but whenever you see a subject line that you think could look good on one of your emails add it to your file then tweak it and use it when appropriate. You can keep your email subject line 'swipe file' in a spreadsheet or this, in my opinion, is the perfect excuse for new notebook (as if I ever needed one).

Having mastered your subject line, it's time to jump into the body of your emails. Join me in the next chapter and we'll pop the bonnet and take a look at the engine.

# The Body of your Email

Well done! You're on the home stretch! We've come a long way so far: we've looked at the reasons why emailing our customers is a good idea, we've explored the different segments of our database and how to build our lists and we've written amazing subject lines to help us get our customers to open emails. In this chapter we'll nail down what it is we want our customers to see when they open our emails. We are going to look at the introduction paragraph, the main body copy of the email and the sign-off (or close) of the email, but before we do I want to touch on a couple of things you *won't* see in an email from me very often.

Firstly you won't see my salon company logo, especially on an email to current customers. The reader should be able to tell who the email is from before they have opened it so they don't need your logo to tell them. While we're on that subject please make sure your emails are setup to send from a human being: my email address is phil@buildyoursalon.com and definitely not messages@, info@ or (my absolute pet hate) donotreply@. If I am going to include a logo it will be small and below the signature line. This is, after all, your customer's email, not your personal ego boost.

Secondly, unless I am illustrating an important point or promoting a specific (and particularly eye-catching) product you won't see many pictures in my emails. Quite simply I like my emails to load quickly on a mobile device and emails which are very heavy with images can be frustrating, especially here where I am writing in deepest Wiltshire where 4G can be almost mythical. Of course, not everyone agrees!

> "Too much text, not enough images ... The secret is to keep your emails visually interesting and include only the text that is necessary."
>
> *Alex Quinn, Phorest*

If you are going to include pictures make sure you have the right to use them as copying an image from Google Images can cause all sorts of legal problems. Look instead to specialist providers like iStockphoto or Shutterstock to make sure you have proper commercial rights. You can, of course, use your own images without worry. Whenever you include a photo give the picture a tagline as these are very often the most-read parts of email.

So how do we get started? Well, here's how I go about it. I write very, very quickly in a kind of frenzied brain dump. I write by hand first and literally throw every idea I have down on paper. Don't edit, don't worry about punctuation, grammar or even putting your thoughts into a logical sequence yet.

Then I take a highlighter pen and pick out the main points I want to communicate. Let's say we are emailing with details of a great new skincare product: I would go through my brain dump and highlight the key reasons this product is great for my customer. Ideally, I would come up with three or four main points, which would then dictate the length of my email.

For a high-profit product or service (and really, why would you email about something with a low profit margin?) I might give each of my highlighted key points a paragraph. For something of a lower value I will try to get all of the points into one or two paragraphs.

Now that I have a target structure for my email I get typing. There is a very old marketing saying which you must bear there in mind while you write: we *sell the sizzle, not the steak.* Don't let your key points be the features of the product unless you can tie those features to a desirable benefit. For example, don't sell me a red hair colour with a new advanced colour molecule, sell me a glorious new shade of sexy red with eye-catching shine that is sure to turn heads.

I do not worry about how long email is yet, I just type it out in the skeleton structure we have come up with. Then, I will edit into a logical order, tidy up the grammar and punctuation and read it through. Usually at this point the email is far too long as I tend to be fairly verbose at the best of times, so it's time to edit down. I take out as many words as I can that add nothing. For example:

> "You'll soon see the terrific results", becomes
> 
> "See terrific results"

I combine short sentences wherever I can and keep reducing and editing to make the whole email snappier and less fluffy. If I'm *really* struggling to hack the email down, I'll choose one key idea or benefit that has to go, but that's as a last resort.

What I *never* do when I'm writing emails is dumb down. There is a lot of talk in copywriting about how you should make your copy readable for an 11 year-old or whatever nonsense is being spouted now. Frankly I think this is rubbish. Keep your customer avatar in mind and talk to them at an appropriate level. If the whole world keeps dumbing down their content and copy we are going to be pitching at a kindergarten level before long. I think the whole concept of dumbing down is insulting at best and disturbing at worst.

Before I finish editing, it's time to put in your calls to action, sometimes called CTAs. You're call to action is what you want your customer to actually *do*. Do you want them to follow you on Facebook? Click this link? Call to book now? Reply to this email?

This is where lots of otherwise-great emails fall short: they forget to ask for the action! It's like being on a dating app where nobody ever "swipes right". Nothing happens! Nothing gets to the next level! Be absolutely clear about what the next step is and you don't just have to ask once either. Depending on the length of your email you can put your call to action in up to three or four times.

> "Every campaign needs a strong call to action."
>
> *Alex Quinn, Phorest*

Your call to action should make it *painfully* easy for your customer and you will get a better response by keeping people on the same platform. Let me explain.

If you ran a Facebook ad asking people to send you a private message you will generally get a better response than asking them to call you as they are already online and in messaging mode. Similarly in email marketing your customer is online so generally you want your call to action to be something they can do online too, or at least from their mobile device. I'm a really big fan of online booking, but speak to your software provider about linking to a *specific service* rather than your general booking page. If you're promoting a spray tan your link needs to take the customer straight to the spray tan booking page, not to a general booking page or to your website.

If your call to action is for the customer to pick up the phone make sure you give your telephone number in full. That way mobile device users can simply touch the number to dial.

Now a personal preference. I don't give alternative calls to action. If my call to action is to follow a link to online booking I won't also give the salon phone number. So in my emails it's one call to action repeated three or four times.

You will get a much better response from the call to action if you can associate it with some kind of scarcity. For example a special offer could have an expiry date or a 'book before' date, you might have a limited number of products at a very special price or you might include a bonus for the first five people to call. Without scarcity there is no urgency, which means your email is in danger of being relegated to the bottom of the list of chores then five days later your customer wonders if she's too late to benefit and doesn't pick up the phone at all.

Next I write my introduction paragraph. If the subject line is there solely to make you open the email, the introduction paragraph is there solely to get you to read on. It should be really simple to read, have a great punch to it and start your customer on a journey down the page.

I very often start my introductions with a really short sentence. Something like this:

> "I admit it."

> "I give up."

> "Did you see it?"

> "This is crazy!"

What we're doing is called "opening a loop" which translates to planting a little bit of unfinished business in the reader's mind to spur them to read on. Your introduction is also the opportunity to close a loop: if you used a blind subject line you need to make it obvious fairly quickly what your email is about or you will annoy your readers.

You do not use the introduction paragraph to sell and this is not a school essay where your opening paragraph needs to be a summary of your email, but it does need to tell the customer what you're emailing them for which is why I find it easier to write the body copy before the introduction.

I like my introduction paragraphs short and snappy and keep them to three or four sentences maximum. I almost always finish the paragraph by opening another loop, to slide the reader into the next paragraph. So I might finish with something like:

> "Here's how."

> "Let me tell you more."

> "But that's not the whole story."

Now we can skip to the end of the email and write our sign-off. You'll have a personal style for this. I finish my emails with a little summary, a repeat of the call to action then and nice light sign-off. I use:

> "Speak soon", or

> "Enjoy the sunshine!" for example.

The sign-off is followed by my name, position and email address.

Then comes the PS. I have no idea why, but the PS is one of the most read parts of your email, so neglect it at your peril. You could put a one-sentence summary and call to action in there, or an extra benefit you think might just tip the scale in your favour. I nearly always repeat the scarcity, for example:

> "There really *are* only 5 available, click here to book now"

Again, a personal thing but I finally go through the email and put the main points I want to highlight in bold text. That way a reader who finds herself in a hurry can scan through your email very quickly and still pick up the three or four main points I wanted her to see.

Then do I press send? Well, no, not usually. I will take an overnight break from my email and come back to it again the next day. You would be amazed by how much polishing you can do with little rest and fresh eyes. Then I check everything twice, I test all the links I've put in and check all the phone numbers, then finally I hit "send". That slight feeling of nausea, by the way, never really goes away. Don't worry, it shows you care.

So congratulations! You've made it to the end! I know this can feel a little daunting: don't worry. I've had some lousy open rates and a ton of unsubscribes over the years but I don't think I've ever lost a salon client through sending an email. There is much to gain and little to lose.

So it's time to get in the game! I really want you to make a start on emailing your customers right away. If you've completed the exercises you will have a pretty good idea on where you want to start by now. If you are really stuck take a look at the downloads section of hairybooks.com/email for a simple two part campaign I've put together for you that you can just amend and send.

DON'T skip the next section! I don't pretend to know all the answers so I have collected interviews with some much cleverer people. I've drawn from their responses throughout this book but it would be an injustice not to print the complete interviews.

I have printed their responses as I received them in full, without editing. They are printed strictly in order of when I received them. Enjoy!

# PART THREE

## The Interviews

# Neil Prigent - Jas Hair

Neil Prigent has worked in the hairdressing industry for the last 10 years working with his wife Jayne within the Multi Award Winning Group JAS Hair. Neil and Jayne have become a leading Salon Group in South Wiltshire and West Hampshire winning Best Local UK Salon twice (2013 & 2015) – Creative Head Most Wanted Awards. They spend time growing their business through their mission statement of enriching the lives of their team, guests and the local community. Neil "works on the business" and Jayne works with the managers and team. Neil says "being able to spend time and plan our marketing, spending time on HR and accounting is something that is so important for any salon business as it gives you the future focus needed to be successful and profitable"

**When did you start emailing your customers? Why did you start? What prompted it?**

We started e mailing guests over 8 years ago as the recession took hold . We wanted to communicate with guests in between their visits and keep them loyal to our Salons rather than the guest seeing the next offer/promotion being advertised from our competitors

**What do you see as the benefits of email marketing for salon businesses? Why should we bother?**

It's a very cheap way of keeping in contact with guests and depending on what you communicate the benefits can be immense. Branding your salon and communicating it can overcome promotions and discounts can create more loyalty

**Have there been any surprise benefits to emailing your customers? Anything you didn't expect?**

Initially when we started we were among the first to do it and clients were impressed with our professionalism along with what is going on in the salon. We needed to ensure our team had all read the newsletter too as clients were talking to them about it!

**Are there any downsides or disadvantages to email marketing?**

I think as a Salon Owner depending how much time you have to spend on working on the business e mail marketing can become a real chore and headache. If not planned well ahead it can be executed badly . Probably a marketing plan is key along with the messages you want to communicate.

**How can email marketing support the other marketing pillars in a small business? How should email integrate with the overall marketing strategy of the company?**

Really important is being consistent across all your media platforms with images, words and messages and therefore a Marketing Plan for the year is crucial and maybe consider outsourcing some of the work as it maybe better to pay someone to do the bits you cant/or don't want to do. The key I think is to have an overriding message and then spread it across your other media platforms

**If a bricks-and-mortar business isn't emailing their customers, should they start? Or is there another direction for marketing you think is more relevant or important?**

It's the marketing mix and in the old days you had a few very simple options for marketing your business today there are loads and you need to be focused on the how and where. E mail marketing for existing guests is important , what about buying a list of e mail addresses to use for new guests ? Online is key and though in the past local papers worked for you they can still do a job on line . Some of the Papers and radio stations have excellent on line presence for advertisers

**How has reaching customers through email changed over the years? How has your strategy altered to allow for these changes? Have any of the changes caught you unawares?**

I was very excited collecting e mails in the early days thinking everyone would read it. As I'm sure you know today we all get hundreds of e mails and it's about content. Also only expect 20%-30% of your e mail list will actually read it and then maybe not all of it. Having collected 1,000 e mail addresses only 200-300 people will read it and that is disappointing though you should still do it!

**What changes do you predict in the coming years? How are you implementing strategies in readiness for those changes? Is email marketing here to stay for the foreseeable future?**

I think software will become more sophisticated with getting our e mails into peoples inbox's and for them to read them. More people will unsubscribe from you too, don't take it personally as they may still be guests of yours ! E Mail will stay for the foreseeable future though I think people will be more fussy about giving out their e mail address. The sophistication of online marketing and how people are targeted with demographics, age etc I think will be part of the future

**Do you use your salon reception system to send emails to your customers or export the data into something else? Why?**

We export our data as our reception system is not sophisticated enough either for newsletter design or reporting . It's also easier to have a separate e mail system if you have contracted that bit of the process out to a third party

**Why do you think so few salon businesses email their customers regularly? What do you think they fear might happen?**

I think many salon businesses are owner driven who also work many hours behind the chair and are unable to take time to think about e mail marketing . I'm not sure fear is the case more about understanding and their time. E Mail addresses need to collected within the salon and that can be difficult if there isn't consistent focus on it

**What needs to change for more salons to take email marketing more seriously? Is it a training issue? An attitude issue? Or a technology issue?**

I think it's the buy in of marketing your business and then how to market it once that has been agreed within the salon. Its easier when the team are all behind it for their benefit

**What strategies have you implemented that a salon could copy to grow their email marketing list? How do you collect email addresses of your customers? What do you do to collect email addresses of potential customers?**

There needs to be a number of ways the salon collects email addresses. On your front page of your website, at reception, any shows you go to, Facebook competitions. The trick is to keep all your e mails in once place, ideally within your salon system. Just about everyone has an email address- mainly due to online shopping and social media! You should be able to collect over 80% of your clients addresses. If you see 1,000 clients a month you should have 800 email addresses and for a salon that size in total over 3,000

**Salons seem to love social media and rather neglect email marketing. Can the two work together? Are there ways for one to feed to other?**

I think practically social media can be a way of collecting email addresses through competitions but you need to be aware of the fact that you need to focus on your target client when these addresses come through. There is no point collecting emails if the type of person will never visit your salon.

**How much email is too much for a customer, do you think? How often do you email your own customers**

There are lots of opinions on this. We email every 4-5 weeks with normally three messages on it. We don't use email for lost clients.

**Is there a reason to stop emailing a lost customer? Or do you think we should keep emailing in they hope they come back one day?**

My view is to continue emailing them until they unsubscribe from the database as that is their choice

**How should we measure the success of our email marketing efforts? What should be monitored?**

This is low cost marketing and should still be measured in terms of open rates in particular. If you have a specific promotion running this can easily be done within the salon.

**What mistakes do you see businesses making in their email marketing?**

I personally don't like too much email from one company and tend to unsubscribe from them. I think too many messages can be lost on a client as well.

**If you were helping a complete beginner to start email marketing, what three things would you teach them?**

- Become a good graphic designer
- Have a marketing plan for 6 months at least
- Research a good online email provider

# Alex Quinn - Phorest

Alex Quinn is a salon marketing specialist at Phorest Salon Software and works with thousands of hair and beauty salons in Ireland, the UK & USA. She has a keen interest in the beauty industry and is the organiser of the Phorest Salon Owners Summit.

**What do you see as the benefits of email marketing for the salon industry? Why should we bother? Are there any downsides or disadvantages to email marketing?**

Email marketing is one of the most efficient, measurable and effective ways to market your salon. It's a way for you to stay in touch with your clients and stay front of their minds. Email marketing also allows you a platform where you can show off your brand, let clients know about special offers or even take online bookings. Except for requiring a little bit of your time, it's the single most inexpensive way of marketing your business.

The downside of email marketing is the fact that nearly everyone does it and it's easy for your message to drown in the sea of marketing emails your clients are receiving. This means you need to put a bit of work & thought into standing out of the crowd and providing value in your content. Make sure the emails are personalised (by that I don't mean writing all 500 of your clients an email, but using an emailing system, like the one within Phorest that will allow you to do this automatically). Be sure to also add something valuable to your email - a pro tip, a how-to video, etc. - together with a good subject line this will help you get your emails opened and read.

**How can email marketing support the other marketing pillars in a salon business? How should email integrate with the overall marketing strategy of the salon?**

Email marketing should absolutely be part of a salon's overall marketing strategy. I do realise that alongside social media and actually working in your salon time for email marketing is scarce. This is why it's especially important to invest in tools that will make your business work better and automate a lot of things without you having to spend hours and hours on creating campaigns & strategies. Collecting e-mail addresses is one of the most valuable things you can do, it's an essential part of not only retaining loyal clients but also building a new client base.

Email is one of the aspects of marketing and you will most certainly not hit all of your salon's demographic with but it's free and can be very effective. Unless you run a business that only caters to 55+, an age group where email is the least effective form of marketing, you will need to dedicate a portion of your marketing efforts to it.

**If a salon isn't emailing their customers, should they start? Or is there another direction for marketing you think is more relevant or important?**

Absolutely! If you have email addresses of your clients, start a monthly email campaign. If you don't have emails another good way of marketing is SMS but you have to be way more creative with your messaging as you only have a very small space to convey your message successfully.

My advice, however, would be to start collecting email addresses immediately! One danger for salon owners and managers, is to think in an 'Email or SMS' kind of way. It is not an either/or, but an integrated campaign is most effect. Always think about how one channel can support the next.

**How important is email marketing in your own business? How often do you email your own customers?**

For us email marketing and content marketing in general are hugely important. We have several people working on email campaigns to our existing clients as well as prospective ones.

Obviously, you can't spam your clients with emails - your goal is to get clients through the door, upsell, keep front of mind and provide value. With this in mind, we as a business, email clients not more than a couple of times a month and target them by interest and opt-in.

## How has reaching customers through email changed over the years? How has your strategy altered?

With the rise of the popularity of email marketing as a channel it is getting more and more difficult to stand out of the crowd and get your message across. We constantly iterate our email marketing strategies, based on testing and the analysis of our campaigns. But ultimately it comes down to staying relevant, providing value to your clients & not spamming them with constant and irrelevant emails.

One thing that has worked well for us is A/B testing email subject lines. For example we will conduct an experiment with a database like so:

"Are you looking to book an appointment Mary?" vs. "Mary, have you heard about our new hair treatment?". The winning campaigns are then uploaded to Phorest Salon Software as email templates so salon owners can benefit from our research.

## Why do you think so few salons email their customers regularly?

Because they are time poor and use the wrong tools. Running a salon business is extremely challenging, especially for those salon owners who alongside managing the business, staff and working with clients, may have to also plan and create email marketing campaigns. It's a lot!

You absolutely cannot afford to let the client experience suffer, staff need attention, stock needs to be ordered in, wages and taxes paid so the first thing that will suffer is the stuff that seems less important. It may seem less important at the time but not investing both time & money into marketing strategies will have negative effects on your business in the long run when you're struggling to fill appointments and generate revenue.

This is, again, why it is so important to have a tool in your salon that will help you spend less time on tasks that add little value to your business and let you concentrate on the things that really matter: providing an excellent client experience, getting your clients through your doors more often, spending more money in your salon.

Also, if salon owners have not been using some best practice techniques, the will see little results, which leaves little desire to do more email marketing.

**What needs to change for salons to take email marketing more seriously? Is it a training issue? An attitude issue? Or a technology issue?**

It's a mix of all of these. Email marketing is not easy and if you're not experienced in it, it definitely requires training. If you don't have the correct technology it becomes practically impossible!

In Phorest we train every single client in email marketing and using the Phorest Salon Software to make it an effective and easy process for people who are essentially not marketing professionals. We also have a team (the Grow Team), who are something like our client's very own marketing agency. They are dedicated to setting up SMS, email and loyalty campaigns to ensure the best effects for our clients.

**How do you define CRM, marketing automation and email marketing? How would you explain the difference?**

CRM is short for Customer Relationship Management and is a strategy for managing a business's relationships and interactions with your customers and potential customers. CRM in the sense of a tool should take care of everything, from marketing efforts, to managing your contacts to sales and financial management.

Marketing Automation, which can be part of some salon CRM / salon software systems, is a technology designed to make it easy to market more effectively on multiple channels (email, social media, blogs) to a large amount of people and automate repetitive tasks.

Email Marketing, in a broad sense, is generating new or repeat business by using emails.

All of the above are very separate terms but are also completely tied into each other. To be able to email market successfully you need marketing automation to some degree, and as a busy salon owner, you will need this as part of a more comprehensive CRM to make the most of the time and money you have available for your marketing efforts.

Many salons have had CRM systems on reception for quite some time - how could they be getting more from those systems? What opportunities do you see being missed? How could salons better use the data they are collecting?

The one single most important thing that often gets missed we see in salons is the failure to collect the client's contact details, specifically their email address and phone number which means they are unable to market to them.

Some salon software systems are also difficult to use making it hard for salon staff to get the best out of them. It is essential to train as much as you can and actually avail of the resources your salon software provider offers. At Phorest our main objective is to see our clients succeed, get more clients and get more money. We achieve this by helping all of our clients using the software to its full potential and giving all clients unlimited training, access to professional teams like the Grow Team and all the support they need.

Our clients are salon owners and their staff, not marketing professionals and it's important for them to choose a salon software provider who understands that and can support their activities in the way they need it.

How much email is too much for a salon customer, do you think?

I think anything more than a monthly email (except for appointment reminders or any other timely announcements) would be too much. Remember, it's all about not spamming your clients!

**Where could salons look for inspiration for content for their emails?**

The Phorest Blog (phorest.com/blog) is a great source of inspiration for email marketing. Our content team puts together campaign ideas for salons and there's even some campaign imagery for download! Phorest clients also have access to a multitude of email templates that contain lots of great campaign ideas.

**Is there a reason to stop emailing a lost customer? Or do you think we should keep emailing in they hope they come back one day?**

In case of a lost customer I don't think they should be emailed the same content as the regular clients. If you are truly trying to get them back in, you will need to reach out with something enticing, a special offer.

Within the Phorest software we actually have a feature, called Client ReConnect, designed to specifically prevent loyal clients from leaving. It automatically tracks overdue clients under each service based upon their own unique booking history and patterns. It then lets you send a ready-made SMS or email message to the client at risk of leaving.

## How should a salon measure the success of its marketing efforts? What should be monitored?

The client retention figure is one of the most important marketing numbers for a salon. If you have the infrastructure to check this, a great thing to check is how many clients are actually booking in appointments after being targeted with an email campaign.

## What mistakes do you see salons making in their email marketing?

Too much text, not enough images. No compelling subject line. No call to action. These are all mistakes we see all the time in salon marketing campaigns. The secret is to keep your emails visually interesting and including only the text that is necessary. And a call to action is extremely important - your aim with every campaign should be centred around achieving a certain result (like filling in next month's appointments, filling seats at a certain time of day, etc.)

## If you were helping a complete beginner to start email marketing, what three things would you teach them?

1    Writing Effective Subject Lines

In order to get your clients to open your marketing emails a compelling and interesting subject line is paramount. This is the first thing your client will see and also the first thing you need to think about when designing a campaign.

2	Writing a Compelling Call to Action

Your marketing campaign is not working for you if it's not achieving the result you set out in the beginning. In order for that to happen every campaign needs a strong call to action.

3	Testing

It may sound a little daunting but testing your content when email marketing is important. Rather than blindly sending emails that you presume are what your clients will respond well to, try gathering data on which subject lines and calls to action got the best open rates and conversion.

## Jo Burgess - Shortcuts

Jo is the VP of Evolution and co-founder of Shortcuts. As one of the key visionaries of this industry-leading salon software brand, Jo has been a driving force behind the business from day one.

As a former salon owner, Jo has an intimate understanding of the unique challenges that affect the hair and beauty industry.

More than 20 years ago, she worked alongside the other founders of Shortcuts to create the world's first touch screen salon software.

Since then, she has seen many technology trends completely reshape the world, and hundreds of new innovations incorporated into Shortcuts' software solution.

Today, Jo continues to provide vision and direction for Shortcuts, and thought leadership for the hair and beauty industry.

**What do you see as the benefits of email marketing for the salon industry? Why should we bother? Are there any downsides or disadvantages to email marketing?**

One of the biggest advantages of email marketing is that you are 100% in control of the message you send out, and who sees it. Compare this with Google Adwords or Facebook, where someone else makes all the rules and even owns all your data! Email really does trump social in our industry – you will get better engagement, and have more control.

If you do it right, email marketing can also be very much a one-on-one tool. By incorporating personalised messages and sending emails at just the right time, you can create engagement on a very personal level. It's easy to target the right people with the right messages, and you can even do it automatically!

I find that email marketing is also the best way to stay in touch with clients in between visits and build a sense of community with stories about your team, your clients and your plans for the future.

A disadvantage of email marketing is that it can be difficult to cut through the clutter in your clients' inbox. You can get around this with a few clever tactics such as incorporating your clients' names in the subject line, keeping content short and snappy, and of course by sending out targeted and timely messages.

**How can email marketing support the other marketing pillars in a salon business? How should email integrate with the overall marketing strategy of the salon?**

Email marketing is an essential part of the marketing mix, you should always think carefully about how it supports the other facets over your overall marketing strategy.

For example, if you are planning on running a promotion over the festive season, you should think about all the different channels you will use to get your message out. Email marketing will play a big part, but chances are social media, in-salon promotional items, and even your staff, will also be critical to the success of your campaign.

Email can achieve what some other channels can't – such as a direct link to your online booking page, prompting people to make an appointment with you asap. This is known as a "call to action" in the marketing world, and it's essential to drive results. There's no point sending out a beautiful email letting your clients know about your latest offer, if they can't then book on the spot.

Your website and social media also go hand in hand with email marketing, and you should always include links on your emails to all of your social media channels and to your website.

**If a salon isn't emailing their customers, should they start? Or is there another direction for marketing you think is more relevant or important?**

If you're not already sending out emails to your clients, you should start today! It's quick and easy, and it can even be completely free if you're just doing the basics.

In the hair and beauty industry we are very lucky to be able to achieve email open rates of around 30% for personalized, targeted and timely emails. Not all industries have this luxury – retail, for example the retails industry's open rates are down around 20%.

Shortcuts offers the ultimate email solution, which is completely automated, so you can set up once and literally let it run year-round, without having to do a thing. Set and forget marketing is connected to your salon database, and will send emails for you, triggered by events and activities such as a client's birthday or the date of their last visit.

**How important is email marketing in your own business? How often do you email your own customers?**

Email marketing is one of the most important channels we use to stay in touch with our customers and build engagement with people who are interested in buying our software.

Each month, we send out around 10 emails, but it's important to note they do not go out to everyone on our mailing list. We pick and choose the right messages for the right audience, and target specific email addresses based on their need, and their relationship with us.

We find this approach produces the best results in terms of high open rates and click through rates, and low unsubscribe rates. In a nutshell, we give people the information we know they are looking for.

**How has reaching customers through email changed over the years? How has your strategy altered?**

Marketing is changing at lightning-fast pace, and email marketing is no exception. Audience needs have changed dramatically – ten or fifteen years ago, when email was new, you could almost guarantee your email would get read. These days, you have to be much more strategic to achieve cut-through.

This involves ensuring emails are more personalised, and are highly visual and engaging. Being mobile-friendly is also a must, as more than 50% of people read their emails on their smartphone. A lot of software systems include drag 'n' drop templates, which make this super easy – it really is simply a matter of dragging and dropping in the content you'd like to include.

Technology will also help you target the right people with the right messages. The best software will do the heavy lifting for you and decide who to email, and when, with which content. Literally, all you need to do it set it up once, and let it work its magic year-round.

**What changes do you predict in the coming years? How are you implementing strategies in readiness for those changes?**

Dynamic content is on-trend right now, and it's only going to get bigger! It might sound like a buzzword, but essentially it lets you set up one email which will show different people different content based on who they are, where they are, what time of day they open the email, and more.

For example, if you know some of your clients regularly visit for beauty services, and some regularly visit for a haircut, you can send them an image that will appeal most to their particular needs.

You can even show different content depending on the weather in their current location!

**Why do you think so few salons email their customers regularly?**

A lot of salons think email marketing is hard work, and they really don't know where to start. If you've never written copy before or done any graphic design, it can seem really scary!

My biggest piece of advice (other than finding the right technology!) for anyone who is feeling like email marketing is just too difficult, is to inject as much personality as they can into what they do.

One common mistake I see is people trying to come across as "professional", which completely dilutes the fact that the hairdressing industry is so much fun!

**What needs to change for salons to take email marketing more seriously? Is it a training issue? An attitude issue? Or a technology issue?**

I think it's a combination of training, attitude and technology. All three are essential to getting good results from your email marketing.

Good software should come with training videos and tutorials to help you really understand how your email marketing works. Once people feel confident with what they are trying to achieve, they will approach things with the right attitude.

The right software will make the entire process easy, with a comprehensive library of industry-specific drag 'n' drop templates that can be customized to suit the brand of each individual salon.

**How do you define CRM, marketing automation and email marketing? How would you explain the difference?**

Your client relationship manager (or CRM) is essentially your customer database, and where all of your transactional activity happens. This is the starting point for all of your marketing activities, so the data should be as clean and accurate as possible.

Marketing automation is broader than just email marketing – these days, you can automate anything from emails to social media to serving up different website content. Again, this relies on having clean data and an accurate idea of who you should target with what message.

Email marketing is exactly what it sounds like – and more! It's the perfect way to communicate in a personalized way and create meaningful engagement with your clients.

**How would you describe the relationship between CRM and email marketing?**

Good email marketing software will let you tap directly into your CRM, so that you can send emails based on information and activities that are stored there. The two systems should talk to each other, so that you can send timely and relevant emails and increase your client engagement.

Having clean data in your CRM is essential to all of this. You can have all the technology in the world, but if you don't have your clients' email addresses you're in a lot of trouble! It's easy to collect this information when they're waiting for their appointment, or when they make a booking.

**Many salons have had CRM systems on reception for quite some time - how could they be getting more from those systems? What opportunities do you see being missed? How could salons better use the data they are collecting?**

As I mentioned above, clean data is key to making the most of your CRM. So many salons have a very powerful piece of technology sitting at their reception desk, which they essentially just use as a glorified cash register. Good software is packed with possibility! Anyone who is interested in growing their business should find out how to use their software to fullest potential – it's not as hard as it can seem!

**What strategies have you seen implemented that a salon could copy to grow their email marketing list?**

The easier you make it for people to give you their email address, the better. When your clients are relaxing in your waiting area, why not hand them an iPad which will let them enter their details directly into your database for you? This saves time and can be much more accurate than using paper forms, then typing this in to your system.

To provide an extra incentive for clients to provide their details, try running a special promo – something like "sign up to our mailing list and win a pamper pack" would work well. You could even get your team on board and offer them some incentives to collect client details too.

**How much email is too much for a salon customer, do you think?**

As a general rule, I would say that you should send no more than two emails a month, and engage via other channels such as Instagram or Facebook. Having said that, it really depends on your overall marketing strategy. If your emails are personal, timely and relevant you can afford to send them more frequently.

For more information on how to create personal, timely and relevant emails, visit www.shortcuts.com.au/quickfix-emails

## Where could salons look for inspiration for content for their emails?

Your inspiration should come from the people around you. Working in a salon, you're surrounded by creative, interesting, fun people all day. Use your team's stories, showcase your clients hair and fashion, and let your clients know about all the fun stuff you have going on.

## Is there a reason to stop emailing a lost customer? Or do you think we should keep emailing in they hope they come back one day?

There's no harm in continuing to email a lost customer – if you engage the right way, and offer them something they are looking for, you may be able to entice them back! Having said that, if a client has opted out from your email marketing, it's really important to abide by the local law in your region. You should always treat people's privacy with utmost respect.

## How should a salon measure the success of its marketing efforts? What should be monitored?

You should always keep an eye on these three key email metrics: open rates, clickthrough rates, and opt out rates. These hold the key to how well your emails are working. High open rates are great, because they mean you have cut through the clutter and that you clients are interested in what you have to say. High clickthrough rates are also important – they tell you your clients want to find out more. High opt outs, on the other hand, are a big warning sign – you are likely to be targeting the wrong people with the wrong messages, and should review your marketing strategy accordingly.

## What mistakes do you see salons making in their email marketing?

The single biggest mistake I see time and time again is poorly designed emails that can't be read on a mobile phone! With more than 50% of people reading emails on their smartphone, it's essential that you make their lives easy by ensuring everything is easy-to-read. It's so easy to create mobile-responsive emails, there really is no excuse!

## If you were helping a complete beginner to start email marketing, what three things would you teach them?

Firstly, always remember – the email you're about to send isn't about what you want, it's about what your client wants.

Secondly, be authentic and have a bit of fun. Thirdly, make it personal, timely and relevant – every time.

# Bart Foreman - Endgame Marketing Solutions

Bart Foreman has formed EndGame Marketing Solutions LLP, a marketing agency that conducts marketing audits and assists clients striving to reach their end game objectives with hands-on marketing management support.

Foreman is no stranger to the beauty industry. He previously founded and owned Group 3 Marketing, a boutique marketing agency that provided forward thinking database driven, marketing focused solutions for all segments of the beauty industry and specialty retailers for almost 30 years.

He co-founded and served as chair of the CRM Special Interest Council of the Direct Marketing Association. He is a frequent speaker at industry trade association meetings, a prolific writer about all things relating to marketing and business growth strategies, and a pioneer marketing thought leader. He is a graduate of the University of Michigan and earned his MBA from DePaul University.

**What do you see as the benefits of email marketing for the salon industry? Why should we bother? Are there any downsides or disadvantages to email marketing?**

I want to begin by redefining the idea of email marketing. There really is no such thing as email marketing. Email is a tool to deliver a salon's message. Staying connected with salon guests is the strategy we want to focus on. The delivery tactic may be postal (snail) mail that costs a lot, texting, phone apps, or social media channels. Email is the most powerful of these tactics but it does not and should not be viewed in isolation.

Why bother? The benefits of a comprehensive marketing program using marketing automation tools to deliver the right message to the right guest through the right channel at the right time is a powerful marketing strategy.

The only downsides or disadvantages to email are not doing it or doing it wrong.

**How can email marketing support the other marketing pillars in a salon business? How should email integrate with the overall marketing strategy of the salon?**

There can be a number of marketing pillars that support the salon and email is the delivery system that will keep the guest connected with the salon. (Note I did not say "keep the salon connected with the guest.) The salon has more than one message to deliver to guests. Using marketing automation, email does this and does it well.

Right from the beginning of the marketing planning process, email should be identified as the #1 communications platform for the salon.

**If a salon isn't emailing their customers, should they start?  Or is there another direction for marketing you think is more relevant or important?**

Yes, start now. If the salon does not have emails, begin collecting them but have a plan in place before asking guests for their information. There are no more important directions than staying connected with guests.

**How important is email marketing in your own business?  How often do you email your own customers?**

As a digital marketing agency, email is very important. I write the Monday Morning INsight, a weekly e-marketing newsletter that goes to clients and prospects.  My agency marketing needs are different than the salon needs but every business needs to stay connected and the timing is critical.

**How has reaching customers through email changed over the years?  How has your strategy altered?**

Looking back, we did business in what I call "The Age of Yesterday." Most communications, whether postal or electronic, were sent once a month and were considered 'batch and blast.' One size, one message fit all guests. Seldom did we bother to shout out a "Thank You," except for holidays or birthdays.

Today, we are doing business in the "Age of NOW!" I created a new salon strategy called Everyday Marketing that is built on transactional data from the POS that is mined nightly. Not everyone is contacted every day, but rather Everyday Marketing connects with guests at the right time with the right message.

The strategy for doing business in the Age of NOW! has become critical because we have learned a lot about the guest journey with the salon. Until recently salons did not understand or really care about the guest journey. New guests need to be on-boarded, active guests need to be thanked for their continued patronage, tomorrow, not whenever. Lost guests need to be reminded to return and a new term we coined a few years ago focuses on "Underperforming guests." These are guests that have not bought at-home care products or specialty add-on services.

Finally, as the guest journey unfolded, we recognized how fragile it really is because at any time in the journey, a guest can become a free agent. It's the task of marketing to minimize defections and staying connected is critical to extending the guest journey.

**What changes do you predict in the coming years? How are you implementing strategies in readiness for those changes?**

The only change I can predict with any accuracy is there will be more changes. Technology will bring new changes. Consumers will change for a variety of evolving social and economic reasons. How that will impact the effectiveness of email as a powerful medium is unknown, but I do not expect the power of email as a delivery channel slipping in the near future.

Why do you think so few smaller salons email their customers regularly?

1. Owners of smaller salons often spend the majority of their time behind the chair and do not have time to create good marketing communications.

2. Small salons do not have the financial resources to execute good guest marketing strategies.

3. Many owners have not been trained to be good business people and do not have the skills to manage a marketing campaign beyond an occasional holiday promotion or a Facebook post.

**What needs to change for salons to take email marketing more seriously? Is it a training issue? An attitude issue? Or a technology issue?**

All of the above. Attitude is probably the most important of the three followed by technology and training. Owners have to embrace the marketing concept that staying connected with guests is vital to strengthening retention and generating new growth avenues. Instead of looking for the cheapest POS vendor, they need to select a POS system that can give them the tools to better understand their business and how to seamlessly connect with their guests. And, owners need to train their staffs to believe that an email address is important to their personal financial growth.

**How do you define CRM, marketing automation and email marketing? How would you explain the difference?**

CRM is the primary marketing strategy to stay connected with guests but many marketing teams have different definitions. Marketing automation is the tool that allows users to target and segment guests to send the right, relevant message to the right guest at the right time. Email is the delivery system.

**How would you describe the relationship between CRM and email marketing?**

They all work together. If the salon does not have a CRM strategy in place, the email campaigns will not be effective.

**Many salons have had CRM systems on reception for quite some time - how could they be getting more from those systems? What opportunities do you see being missed? How could salons better use the data they are collecting?**

Too many owners do not take advantage of the tools that their POS systems have. They either do not have time, have not been trained, or just don't care. There are multiple missed opportunities to exploit email schemes. Some POS marketing platforms are better than others and when a salon considers a new system, this should be an important focal point.

In terms of using the data better, owners need training on how to mine the data to better understand their guests. Who are high value versus low value guests and why is this important? Most owners do not realize that the average salon has about 27%-30% of their guests who spend above the annual average and this group accounts for about 70% of annual revenue. Most salons do not realize that almost 50% of their guests are low value and account for 10% of their annual sales. Once a salon understands the METRICS of their business, they can implement strategies to connect with guests in a relevant way.

**What strategies have you seen implemented that a salon could copy to grow their email marketing list?**

Rewards. Creating an electronic version of the old punch card rewards program is an excellent initiative to encourage guests to give their email address. Add to that special offers and "Bonus Point" promotions and the guest becomes much more open to giving the email address. The other part of this approach is to promise that the salon will not send too many emails because hair only grows so fast and that the salon respects the guest's privacy.

**How much email is too much for a salon customer, do you think?**

As noted above, hair only grows so fast. That model might change a little if the operation includes a spa with additional services. This basic marketing automation system we have traditionally recommended is (1) a Welcome email the first time the guest is entered into the POS, (2) a thank you email after each visit (showing how the guest is progressing to the next reward), A reminder if no activity (hair only salon) after 45 days, (3) a follow-up after 60 days, and a third follow-up after 75 days. Additional messages with appropriate promotional offers/discounts should be added at 120 days and 150 days. Add a color reminder 55 days after the last color service, and appointment reminders 10 days before the next appointment and again the day before. Those are what we call the basic marketing automation "triggers."

**Where could salons look for inspiration for content for their emails?**

Very critical. The inspiration comes from studying the salon's website and then talking with the salon to better understand "the voice" of the salon. A professional agency person should take the lead in writing content. For trigger emails, the content should be very short and relevant. Use pictures whenever possible and engage guests by highlighting team members, their training and their expertise.

**Is there a reason to stop emailing a lost customer? Or do you think we should keep emailing in they hope they come back one day?**

There is a point of no return. As noted above, we generally will go out about 4 or 5 months and then stop. The last email usually has a one or two question survey. (1) Why have you not come back and (2) an open ended comments section. We encourage some kind of incentive to bribe the former guest. Usually a coupon to a local coffee house. We do not recommend a salon service discount because if they have not previously returned they probably will ignore the survey.

**How should a salon measure the success of its marketing efforts? What should be monitored?**

If the salon implements a digital email marketing automation program, it should measure the growth of email addresses and then measure retention and sales growth of guests with email that are being contacted versus those with no email addresses. Measure guest activity, sales growth and average time between visits. Also, make a specific effort to measure those guests who only come in once and watch to determine if that percentage of total guests is declining as the email campaigns expand.

## What mistakes do you see salons making in their email marketing?

1. If they do any emailing it is a monthly "Batch and Blast" once in a while or as some say, "Spray and Pray."
2. Owners/managers do not make it a priority to stay connected with their guests.
3. Owners do not focus on the marketing metrics of the salon.

## If you were helping a complete beginner to start email marketing, what three things would you teach them?

1. Why staying connected with timely relevant messaging is so important to the survival of the salon.
2. Why a rewards scheme is an integral element of the program.
3. How a digital marketing initiative will help their business grow.

# Chris Davis - ActiveCampaign

Chris Davis is currently the Director of Education at ActiveCampaign, where he is responsible for the organization and creation of content to provide business owners the instruction they need to properly utilize marketing automation. With over 12 years of professional experience in the technology and business space, he is passionate about helping companies grow by use of technology in their marketing.

**What do you see as the benefits of email marketing for small brick and mortar businesses. Why should we bother, are there any downsides or disadvantages to email marketing?**

Stats have shown that fortune is in the follow up, and most brick and mortar stores are used to doing some form of manual follow up; this is limited to the amount of people they can hire, and limited to the amount of time those people have. When you include things like email marketing, it allows you a way to better follow up and nurture visitors to your store that have not bought, or to turn customers into repeat buyers. There are things you can do with email that are very valuable, very low cost, and low time intensive. For example, sending them a coupon for their next purchase, or perhaps a seasonal offer. Email allows you a direct line of communication to those who have expressed interest in your products and/or services. You can also run events; you can use email marketing to target people within a certain demographic and let them know, "hey we're coming to your area."

If we change the words "email marketing" and replace it with "a direct line of communication to your consumers," it becomes a little easier to understand the benefits and why you should bother using it.

Now, the downsides come from not knowing how to do email marketing, and over-usage: the downside to anything is abuse. For those who know how to use email, I would say, you perhaps sacrifice the personal touch. You can rely too heavily on email in instances where you should have reached out to them personally; but again, this is in the case of misuse of email marketing, which comes from a lack of education and understanding.

Remember this is just another tool, another strategy, a follow up: that's what email marketing should be.

**How can email marketing support other email marketing pillars in a small business? How should email integrate with overall marketing strategy for the company?**

You can support it by getting people in the door, and returning back to the door.

It's been said that a lead takes seven touches before they convert to a customer. I think that's increased honestly; I think we're closer to fourteen or seventeen. I think it's doubled due to the information age.

Given the abundance of information we're bombarded with, you can never get enough eyes on what you have to offer. So, when you're sending emails (of course no email marketer is never going to send an email that doesn't have a link in it), and when someone clicks on that link, that gives you the opportunity to get one of those views. If it's going to take seventeen, perhaps email marketing can cover seven of them. That's seven less things you have to worry about. Maybe you don't have to pay for that radio ad that's going to get you seven touches, because email marketing is taking care of that for you.

On the sales end, you should send coupons, send offers, send updates on events, send news; whatever it is that supports what you're doing in your business.

Everything should feed into your CRM. Your email marketing platform should house all of the action, all of the behaviour that your contacts take on the email. It should have that information stored and ready to initiate some form of action to help fully execute your marketing strategy. It should also tie into your payment processor. There's no reason why someone buying your product should not be able to be traced back to the email that generated that purchase.

**If brick and mortar businesses aren't emailing their customers, should they start or is there another direction for marketing you think is more relevant?**

The return on investment for every dollar spent in email marketing is about $44. There's no reason why you should not be sending an email. Other marketing efforts include retargeting or remarketing.

Let's just say someone visited your site for hair conditioner: they were very concerned about hair condition, and they visited your site, but they didn't buy. So now you, a savvy marketer, you're doing some retargeting on Facebook, and you're putting pictures of all of these women with great hair that have used that conditioner. It's going to be very hard for you to get the sale on Facebook, by using disruptive means of marketing like that.

However, what if that ad said get $10 off? If you're going to disrupt my normal browsing behaviour, at least give me something for it; and in order to get that $10 off, I just need to give you my email address. I give you my email address, and the email you send me is the coupon. That's why you should be using email: it works in conjunction with so many other of your marketing efforts. This is an inclusive approach instead of exclusive.

Email marketing is a mutually inclusive strategy. It's not like you have to give up one to perform the other. You can do both.

**How has reaching customers through email changed over the years, how has your company strategy altered to allow these changes. Have any of these changes caught you unaware?**

No, I have not been caught unaware. What's changed over the years is it's harder to get into your inbox; Gmail and Yahoo and Outlook are now looking, they're just waiting to mark you as spam, because other people have abused email marketing.

Email is more easily adaptable and accessible to the lower end of the market; that enables some to abuse it at a high rate, which hurts everyone, and requires that we (the ones who send responsibly) do our due diligence in researching how to make sure we're offering something that's aligned with the needs of our audience. So if our email does end up in the spam, that person wants your communication so badly, that they'll go and check their spam for that email. This speaks to their true desire for your product or service.

So yes, it's become increasingly hard to land in the inbox over the years, for those who aren't aligned with their customer base and highly engaged with them.

What we've done at ActiveCampaign to circumvent this, is train, teach, and provide tools for you to be the most responsible email sender. So, you can do things in our platform like track the web pages people have visited, you can track what emails they've opened, what links they've clicked, and what forms they filled out. All of this information is used to help segment your database so you can send targeted emails to people, and those targeted emails are going to avoid the spam box. They are going to get high open rates, high click rates, and result in highly effective communications. We provide you with tools to segment your list, and get laser sharp with your focus, and get the right message, to the right people, at the right time.

**What changes do you predict in the coming years, how are you implementing strategies in readiness for those changes. Is email marketing here to stay for the foreseeable future?**

Email marketing is going nowhere. We're just going to continue to build: it's not going anywhere. We're just going to continue to build on its effectiveness. So, perhaps it's harder to land in the inbox now, but that doesn't mean that you should stop sending. It is still an effective means of communication, because you can reach somebody and they can listen to you without noise. I can read an email anywhere, and your message is communicated with me, and I can take action without having to be heard or seen.

The changes I see in the coming years is evolution; there's going to be multiple forms of messaging, it's not going to be just limited to your inbox. There are going to be other means of providing that direct one-on-one communication, or one-to-many communication, in more ways than just your inbox.

Here at ActiveCampaign, site messages prove this to be true. You can now turn your website into an inbox by having messages appear on your website, just like you would have in your email. So again, different forms of messaging. Both messages are going to leverage each other, because perhaps you go to my website and see a message that says "Hey! $10 off!" instead of seeing an ad on Facebook. If you're on my website I can already assume that you're interested, and then perhaps while you're there you can say "Yes! I want $10 off." Well you're going to submit your email address, and again we see that email becomes the foundation all the other efforts are built on: it's your failsafe. At a bare minimum, you need to be able to send emails. Everything else builds on top of that.

**Your company has customers across the world, do you see any differences in the way businesses use email in different countries. Do customers respond differently to email marketing?**

You know what, I don't see any differences. I would say the more advanced, the more progressive the countries that are using technology are, the more email usage would increase, but it's like asking me whether calling habits are different here than in another country. It really depends on the complexity of the technology in that country, but if it's just as available as it is in the US, the trends are going to be similar. I call somebody in the US the same way I will call somebody in Europe or Australia, that doesn't change. What changes is the time of day, and their availability, and their access to such technology. So as long as those things are constant, if technology is there, email marketing provides you a means of communicating with them by using technology, but it's not specific to a country.

The country-specific aspects are access to internet, and access to technology that can help you leverage email marketing; that's what would have the biggest impact.

But customers, the response - people respond to engagement, people respond to people who get them, who understand them, who they feel have something to offer to them. That's what people respond to, not email marketing. Email marketing is the means, the venue, it is not the thing. Your business is the thing. If people like what you're doing, and they like you, and they want to engage with you, email marketing just provides a means for them to do that conveniently.

**Why do you think so few smaller businesses email their customers regularly?**

Simple answer, they don't know how to. I'm not talking down on the business owner, a lot of savvy established businesses do not know how to email their customers regularly.

If I asked you how would you talk to a customer, you wouldn't have much of a problem figuring that out. But the second I put technology between you and the customer, things get foggy. And they shouldn't, because email is no different than a letter in the mail or a postcard that you send: it's not different.

The means is what is different, it's technology instead of a piece of paper, but there's no reason why you can't use email in the same form. It's a lack of understanding that comes from the small barrier or the amount of uncertainty technology introduces.

If a business owner is savvy in running their business but doesn't understand technology, they're going to struggle with email marketing. Not that they don't understand the power of nurturing, they understand how necessary it is to follow up with your leads. They understand all of that, but the inclusion of technology confuses them. So, often, I personally spend time translating what they would do in person to the computer or technology. That's why so many businesses don't do it, because they don't have a translator, nor do they have the ability to understand technology and email marketing at the same level that they understand just regular marketing.

**What needs to change for more businesses to take email marketing more seriously, is it training in attitude or technology?**

I would say it's all of the above. It's the lack of accurate education and training out there that makes it difficult. It makes it hard for somebody to figure out how to do email marketing when there are so many people in the space, with apparent scamming efforts or get-rich-quick schemes.

There's a lot of barriers honestly, so I look at it as a training issue, a technology issue, and an attitude issue. However, for brick and mortar based businesses that have access to a local consultant, or a company like yours that values education, and where they can gain that understanding, perhaps they can couple that understanding with a consultant who can execute it for them.

I think you'll see a lot more businesses take email marketing seriously, because once it's implemented correctly they'll start getting results and they'll never minimize that impact again. But, it's going to require some education, some awareness, some understanding, as well as someone who understands technology, to do it for them. It's a fallacy to think that a business owner is going to learn this stuff and do it; it's just not reality. The business owner needs to understand that it's a great opportunity to invest in, and generate more dollars for the business, but then they need someone on the marketing team, they need a technician to learn how to do it, and be educated with the proper steps. You have those two things in place, and trust me they'll take it a lot more seriously.

**How do you define CRM, marketing automation and email marketing?**

Email marketing exists within marketing automation. In fact, you could say that the difference between email marketing platforms and marketing automation platforms is the inclusion of a CRM – a Contact Relationship Management system.

In email marketing, people are just an email address; that's how you identify who they are. If they don't have an email address, they don't exist, because the whole point of email marketing is to send email. When you move over into marketing automation, maybe I don't care about your email: maybe I need to know your age, your phone number so I can call you, your gender and your income. For example, if I'm an insurance company.

So, these leads are going to exist in my database and I may not email them, I may strictly call them. That brings us to another difference, because not only is the inclusion of a CRM a difference, but there is back end automation that can happen now. The highest form of automation that can happen in email marketing is the automating of sending emails: that's it. You can't automate anything else. Marketing automation, on the other hand, encompasses email and much more.

You can automate across a much larger portion of your business; you can automate the sales process, you can automate the back-end fulfilment processes, you can automate more of the front-end processes. And if you find that you don't need more than an email address, you're not collecting data on your contacts, that's your first sign that you don't really need CRM. If you don't need a CRM, there's a good chance you don't need marketing automation. However, if you're collecting data about your contacts over time, and you're reaching out to them in multiple ways besides just email, you're going to want to leverage marketing automation. You have to for your own sake.

**Which strategies have you seen implemented that a Salon can copy to grow their email marketing list?**

One of my favourites is online scheduling. There is absolutely no way every salon across the country, across the world, should not be offering online scheduling. And if you want to take it a level up, you offer online scheduling per staff member, so each staff member has their own calendar. Now, someone no longer has to call in, they can go on the website, and schedule some time with you.

Another one is a check-in kiosk, so when people come in, you have them sign in - name, number, email, click "check in".

You could have your marketing automation platform take that check-in data and run some actions. But, more importantly, what you can do when they check-in and give you their phone number, you can now send them an SMS reminder to schedule their next appointment, if they haven't scheduled it on their way out. You could email them a discount for their next haircut, all from a kiosk that captures their name and email. And if you already have their name and email, it will just capture the last time that they were in your store. And maybe you have some intelligent marketing automation around every time somebody checks in, and if they don't check in within two weeks, you flag that they may be slipping through the cracks.

So perhaps you automatically send them an email, "Hey haven't seen you for a while, it's been a couple of weeks," but if they do check in within two weeks, that email doesn't go out. Just these examples alone get me excited, because these are processes that are critical to a salon, and right now you either have an administrative assistant doing it all, or you, the Owner, is doing it all, or people are simply slipping through the cracks, and you're relying more heavily on word of mouth and flyers to do the marketing and getting people back in the door for you, which is not as effective.

**Salons seem to love social media and neglect email marketing. Can the two work together, are there ways for one to feed into the other?**

Every social media effort should be coupled with email marketing, because you can only go so far with just social. You can only have a certain level of conversation on social media. I like comparing it if you're in a club: if you're at a club and it's loud and you like somebody, you're only going to be able to talk so much with those loud speakers and people dancing all over the place. So, at some point you want to take that conversation to a quiet space that's a little more intimate so that you can get to know somebody better. What's that quiet space online? The loud space is social media: everything is going on - pictures, video's, statuses. It's just loud, but where's that quiet place? The quiet place is the email inbox.

That's the place that you take them to and get to know them better, so every effort on social media should provide a pathway for that quiet communication to take place, which is the email inbox.

So, they should work together, and again, I can't get rid of this both-end approach. They're not mutually exclusive, you don't have to stop doing one to do the other. They feed each other so well that when you set it up right, you'll be amazed and elated at the results that you're receiving. You should never do one without the other: social media amplifies your brain, it puts it in front of more people than email ever could. Use social media to amplify, to build a following, get your message out there, but once it's out there you need to capture those people. You do that by getting their email addresses, taking a conversation offline, in the email box. That's intimate, quiet and individualised.

**How much email is too much for a customer do you think. How often should you email your own customers?**

This is a very subjective question, because it really depends on the business. So, I'll try and answer it as objectively as possible, and the good rule of thumb I have is email as much as you need to. I have businesses where I email every day. I've worked with other businesses that email once a month, others email once a week. It's really up to you to see what is your consumer base requesting from you. If they're requesting more communication bump it up!

If it's ongoing communication you probably don't want to send that through email. You don't want to send somebody an update everyday of what you're doing new. Maybe you should use social media for the day to day stuff and then use email for maybe a weekly or monthly digest of everything that's been happening in your company. If you're often running promotions or events, you'll want to probably send emails more frequently.

But again, coupling email with other resources like social media, like Facebook groups, online forums, is a very powerful one-two punch. For updates, day-to-day stuff that perhaps you don't want to send in an email, you can use email to say "Hey this is what you may have missed this month" and it links to everything that you've done. So emailing a customer is really dependent on how frequently they want to hear from you, and how engaged they are with your brand.

**How should we measure the success of our email marketing efforts, what should be monitored?**

You measure the success by sales: that's it. Anything with the word 'marketing' attached to it, it should be held up to a microscope of 'are you generating revenue?'

Marketing primarily is used to generate money, and if it's not generating money it's not effective. You should monitor open rates: the open rates will let you know the level of interest that somebody has. The click rate of an email will measure the amount of intent they have. ActiveCampaign allows you to see trends, which days are people opening up your emails more, what time of the day, which devices: these are things are important. But when you're starting out, you want to measure your opens and your clicks, because they'll tell you interest and intent.

**What are the common mistakes you see business make in their email marketing?**

Sending an email just to send it: somebody told them to send an email so they send an email. You have no strategy, you really don't know what you're doing.

People putting a "give me your email" web form on your website, with no clarity on what someone gets from it. "Join my newsletter": there's no description of what your newsletter is, what you'll be sending, how frequently you'll be sending it, and it you're not setting an expectation up front. Then you're bound to be marked for spam, and be punished.

Another common mistake: too many images. An email is not a web page: you do not need to put big images or too many images. Every piece of media you add to an email is going to increase the chances that it's marked as spam, it's just what it is. Text-based emails perform the best. So, trying to go too heavy on the design is another one. Lastly, having no call-to-action. You should never send an email just to say "Hi". You have to respect people's inbox: this is their time they're giving you. When they open your email, you just bought their attention which is very valuable, so don't abuse it by sending something just to say "Hi," take them somewhere. Have them click on a link, and provide value.

**If you were helping a complete beginner to start email marketing, what three things would you teach them?**

The first thing I would teach them is to have a strategy, and the importance of starting with the end goal. If the end goal is a product, or an attendance to an event, or more demos booked, that gives me a target to hit. That gives me a means of measuring the effectiveness of my emails. Once we strategize and identify my goal, I will then work backward and come up with something to offer that is aligned with the end result. If it's a product, such as shampoo, maybe I want to offer a quick cheat sheet of the five benefits to your hair and just give it away. Maybe it's a video series, maybe it's a PDF download; whatever it is I'm going to give it away and it's going to be aligned with my product. So, the first thing is creating a strategy that begins with the end goal.

Once I know the end goal, I'm going to create something that I can provide on the front end that's absolutely free but ties into my product.

The third thing is to write emails that connect the dots for contacts. I'm going to take what I gave for free, and I'm going to draft some emails that give a little more explanation on exactly how your hair will never be the same. And after we've done that, you would have essentially completed your first email funnel or campaign, and you'll feel great about it.

# ACKNOWLEDGEMENTS

HUGE THANKS to my contributors: incredibly busy people who gave up their time to help improve our wonderful industry. None of them were paid for their contributions and it's humbling that such icons still find time to give.

ONCE AGAIN lots of gratitude and respect to the gorgeous team at Bravo Hairdressing: you really are my rock and I adore you all.

A BIG DOLLOP of thanks to Adam Turner from Shortcuts who has been insanely supportive with this project for no returns (except champagne). You should read his blog … ;)

AS ALWAYS love to the wonderful salon industry for being superb, creative and flirty, but this time I'll add the software chaps to the mix who have been patient when I've asked some very dumb questions. Quite a lot less flirty though.

EXTRA BEAR HUGS to my Build Your Salon mentoring clients who help no end with my research and always inspire through their willingness to grow.

LONG DISTANCE thanks to Janet Keiser in SA who I've never met but can transcribe the hell out of anything.

GREAT BIG LOVE to my husband Scott who keeps me going when I'm ready to throw in the towel and get a proper job. PLUS he makes a lovely brew.

AND FINALLY to my boys. Thanks for all the hugs. xx

# SPECIAL OFFERS - WORTH £674!

## ANYTHING ELSE I CAN HELP WITH?

It's not just email. I have helped salons across the world with a whole range of business issues.

My mentoring clients are a mix of hair and beauty salon owners and managers who have regular calls with me to set targets, ask for advice and make plans for growing their business and profits. Sound good?

Get a FREE preliminary consultation worth £74 on the topic of your choice. Head to hairybooks.com/consult to book your free slot.

## WANT MORE HELP WITH EMAIL MARKETING?

When writing a book like this, it's hard to know how to pitch it. I hope there's something for everyone in here, but I also know there are larger salons and businesses that need more tailored help than I can give here.

I hate to leave anyone hanging and it is literally my job to help! Head over to hairybooks.com/consult and you can **save £600 on my daily consulting rate for email marketing!**